Sir Michael Sadler

A bibliography of his published works

D1824204

O. S. Pickering

LEEDS STUDIES
IN ADULT AND CONTINUING EDUCATION

First published in 1982 in the series
Leeds Studies in Adult and Continuing Education
by the University of Leeds, Department of
Adult and Continuing Education
Leeds LS2 9JT

Leeds Studies in Adult and Continuing Education
ISSN 0261–1406

Sir Michael Sadler: a bibliography of his published works
ISBN 0 907644 01 5

Set in 10 point Times Roman
and printed in Great Britain by J. Jackman and Co.
Chancellor Street, Leeds LS6 2TG

Acknowledgments

This bibliography was first suggested to me in March 1978 by Dr J. H. Higginson, at the time when he was preparing his anthology, *Selections from Michael Sadler* (1979). I have benefited enormously from his enthusiasm and unrivalled knowledge of Sadler's writings, and from his generosity to the Brotherton Library in depositing a substantial proportion of his own collection of Sadler's papers, both printed and unprinted, the whole of which is eventually to come to the Library. I have also enjoyed the constant encouragement of the Librarian, Mr D. Cox, who was happy for me to go in pursuit of Sadleriana away from Leeds, and the advice and assistance of the librarian-in-charge of the Education Library, Mr J. R. V. Johnston.

I did not have to begin the task of compiling the bibliography from scratch, for I was able to draw on earlier listings by Dr Higginson, in his Leeds Ph.D. thesis, 'The contribution of Sir Michael Sadler to the study of comparative education' (1955); by Dr J. S. Andrews (a former education librarian at Leeds and now Sub-Librarian at the University of Lancaster), in the handlist of printed material at Leeds issued in 1968; and by Mr A. J. Edwards (Tutor-Librarian of Christ Church College, Canterbury), in *Gleanings for tomorrow's teachers,* a pamphlet published by the College in 1971. Professor J. Sislian of the University of Hamburg, Dr J. S. Marriott of the Department of Adult Education and Extramural Studies at Leeds, and, of course, Dr Higginson, have told me of items that I would otherwise have missed. I have tried to examine personally as many items in the bibliography as possible, but I am glad to acknowledge the help of the following people and libraries with checking details: Miss Claire Drinkwater of the University of London Institute of Education Library; Mr C. J. Gibson; Dr Elizabeth James of the British Library Reference Division; Mrs E. Parkinson, formerly of the John Rylands University Library of Manchester; Dr David Thistlewood; Mr A. J. Trump, Librarian of the Department for External Studies, University of Oxford; Miss E. M. Willmott of Bradford Central Library; the British Library Newspaper Library; Manchester Central Library; and Oxfordshire County Library. The British Library of Political and Economic Science, the Director of Education for Guernsey, the Secretary of the National Froebel Foundation, the Library of Trinity and All

Saints College, Leeds, and the Library of the Victoria and Albert Museum willingly supplied me with photocopies, and Mrs J. Macrory, the Librarian of Rugby School, kindly lent me an annotated set of the school magazine for 1877–78. For granting me special access to manuscripts, indexes, and other materials in their care, I am especially grateful to the Bodleian Library, the Department of Education and Science Library, the John Rylands University Library of Manchester, Yorkshire Post Newspapers Ltd, and the custodians of the University of Leeds Archives. The work would have taken far longer to complete had I not been able to make constant use of the Brotherton Library's own rich resources.

I am grateful to the editors of Leeds Studies in Adult and Continuing Education for including the bibliography in their series, to the University of Leeds for publishing it, and to Dr Marriott for contributing a biographical introduction. Mrs Norma Hines typed the penultimate and final drafts with remarkable devotion in the midst of other duties. I should also like to thank my colleagues at the Brotherton Library's inter-library loans desk for cheerfully coping with my demands upon them.

O. S. Pickering

June 1982

Contents

Biographical introduction

by Stuart Marriott

At the very beginning of his career Michael Sadler achieved a degree of prominence, as one of the most important figures in 'University Extension' and mastermind of Oxford's contribution to that remarkable movement for spreading higher education beyond the walls of universities. A man of his abilities and energy, and consuming interest in the great issues of public policy, could not be content in what was, unhappily, the back-water of adult education; he was cut out for greater things and indeed held office, between 1911 and 1923, as Vice-Chancellor of the University of Leeds. So it is particularly appropriate that Oliver Pickering's *Bibliography* of Sir Michael Sadler's multitudinous writings should now be published in his adopted University and by collaboration between the Library (which holds an extensive collection of his works) and the series of Leeds Studies in Adult and Continuing Education.

Only a small proportion of the work identified by Dr Pickering, in the main produced before 1895, is concerned with adult education pure and simple, but everything Sadler did publish in that period is important to an understanding of the development of early university adult education. Sadler left Oxford in 1895, when he had already begun to establish himself as an authority on the government of education, particularly as it affected secondary schooling and the training of adolescents; the many official and semi-official reports he subsequently produced on those topics have become part of the corpus of educational history. But, as several of Dr Pickering's entries reveal, he did not turn his back on adult education, a movement which for him was a part of the history of social progress in nineteenth- and early twentieth-century England. He and his contemporaries in University Extension worked on ideas that we rashly assume to have been invented by the 'continuing education' theorists of our own day. In later years he retained the conviction that education was a deeply formative influence which must address itself to the whole community, not just to those in schools and colleges.

During Sadler's time at Leeds a local magazine found itself in near-bewilderment at the number and variety of his academic and public

engagements; it decided that only a cartoon-sketch could do him justice, and added by way of caption: 'our artist was constrained to wonder how it was done ... for physical and mental activity combined, the probability is that the Vice-Chancellor has not at present a peer in the West Riding'. In an introduction to a study published as part of a series in adult and continuing education there is naturally a temptation to draw attention selectively to one area of Sadler's physical and mental activity. What matters of course is the variety of his involvements, whether at a particular date or across his whole career.

This bibliography is an important resource for anyone who needs to come to terms with Sadler, in his total personality or in any of his particular activities. The list of his involvements is an impressive one: adult and then secondary and further education, with the development of international comparative studies thrown in for good measure; consultative work in the early years of the local education authorities created by the Act of 1902; Leeds University in a significant period of development; reorganisation of higher education in Bengal; the defence of Oxford's buildings and open spaces against the impositions of the twentieth century. On the more personal side was his patronage of art, particularly of post-impressionist painting. In most of the areas where Sadler set foot the results were such that the historian must take account of them.

Michael Ernest Sadler was born on 3 July 1861 at Barnsley in the West Riding of Yorkshire. He came from a lively middle-class, professional family, and was pleased to be able to list the Michael Thomas Sadler of the factory-reform movement among his antecedents. He was at school at Rugby, where he became head of his house, showed a somewhat impulsive earnestness, experienced the pangs of a progressive social conscience, and saw his words in print for the first time.

In 1880 he went up to Trinity College, Oxford to read *Literae Humaniores*. Sadler found himself one of a particularly brilliant undergraduate generation and soon figured among its leaders. His friends and acquaintances included many who were to become eminent in the country's political and intellectual life. As students most of them were influenced by the heady philosophy of 'practical idealism' cultivated by

the neo-Hegelian T. H. Green and his disciples. John Ruskin's personal presence and ideas about art and social morality attracted much attention in the Oxford of those days; Sadler listened and admired. He began to think of himself as a 'socialist'. More inspiration came from Arnold Toynbee, and when he was gathered into a select conversation club presided over by another Greenite, A. H. D. Acland, a friendship began which was to prove very important to his later career. Most of his circle were advanced Liberals or Radicals; they created a progressive inter-regnum in the affairs of the Oxford Union, and Sadler took his turn as President of that Society. He belonged also to the group which founded the *Oxford Magazine* and imposed on it a character of almost solemn social responsibility.

Sadler obtained the passport to eminence — presidency of the Union and a first in Greats — but after graduating B.A. he was unable to find congenial employment. Part of the problem was that he had come under the spell of Acland's enthusiasm for the educational possibilities of the co-operative movement and was much attracted by the prospect of some kind of itinerant, missionary lectureship to the societies in the North of England. Connected with this proposal was the decision to revive Oxford's dormant committee for university extension lectures, and in April 1885 Sadler's position was made clear by Acland's decision to resign the secretaryship and hand it on to the younger man. Sadler assumed sole responsibility for Oxford's extramural lectures work when he was twenty-three years old. For the next decade he was prodigiously active and successful as Extension Secretary (and in order to make a decent income he also contrived to work as Steward, or junior bursar, of Christ Church).

By 1890 he had transformed the Oxford branch from sleeping partner into dominant voice in the Extension world. His methods were unorth-odox and sometimes became a focus of considerable hostility from those already established in the field. He evolved the doctrine that the primary aim of his work was to extend the moral influence of Oxford University throughout the country — and, by visiting the United States and fostering contacts there, to America too.

Some of his particular activities may be mentioned. He was the first to take really seriously the idea that central government should give financial support to University Extension, and had the subsequent campaign for 'state aid' succeeded the history of adult education might

have been very different. Because of his contact, through Acland, with the technical education lobby, Sadler pushed the Oxford Extension committee into a very substantial involvement in 'intermediate' technical courses under the provisions of the Local Taxation Act of 1890 (an example energetically followed by Cambridge). This success was short-lived and the policy became discredited, yet its author was already showing a precocious aptitude in statesman-like discussion of the country's wider educational problems. Leaving aside the building of a very large programme of regular Extension lectures, Sadler's most conspicuous achievement was that, together with his colleague Halford Mackinder, he revived the notion of the 'local college' (long associated with the Extension movement) and did much of the work in setting up a University Extension College at Reading, a humble foundation which was to become a university in its own right.

At the peak of these early successes, about 1892–93, Sadler became unhappy about his position at Oxford. He had refused a lucrative offer from the *Manchester guardian* for the sake of his Extension work, but began to feel over-burdened and was chafing at the University's refusal to give the kind of financial support needed for a secure administrative and staffing structure. Furthermore the experience of improvising valiantly on the margin of the educational system demonstrated that University Extension was not able to achieve the influence he sought for it, and so was no really adequate response to the problem of English education. In 1893 he agitated for and then organised a major conference on secondary education, held at Oxford, and one result was that in 1894 the government was persuaded to appoint a commission of inquiry. Acland, who had gone into politics and was virtually minister for education, sponsored Sadler, now aged thirty-three, as a member of the Royal Commission on Secondary Education, and his protégé played an important part in its deliberations. A year later Sadler gave up adult education for good when Acland, in the dying days of the Liberal government, invented for him the post of director of the Office of Special Inquiries and Reports in the Education Department.

It is impossible to offer a reassuringly rounded summary of the first phase of Sadler's career in education. He registered considerable achievements, but in cutting a dash as a public figure he also sometimes indulged his impulsive enthusiasms, and relations with colleagues occasionally showed a lack of wisdom and generosity. His successor at the

Extension office felt that the results had not always been to the University's credit and resolved on a more orderly approach to the task.

There was also ample evidence of a peculiarity of temperament that was to persist throughout his life, a combination of boyish enthusiasm and high-mindedness which his friends found irresistible and his enemies considered shallowness or pretence. The economist L. L. Price mischievously recalled many years later that in undergraduate days some detected more than a hint of 'humbug' about his fellow Trinity man. Yet it was also Price who recorded that most of his circle believed that Sadler would go into politics and end up as Prime Minister. Even in these early days Sadler's work brought him into touch with men of considerable influence, and those who warmed to him warmed completely. For many years people, some with seats at their disposal, were to press him to go into Parliament.

In an essay published in 1901 (no. 80 in the bibliography) Sadler argued that the mid 1880s had been a period of critical confrontation between *laissez faire* and a more 'scientific' approach to organising society. As one of the new Liberals, evolving his own blend of socialism, meritocracy, efficiency and cultural enlightenment, Sadler was himself part of that confrontation. The move to the Education Department promised greater scope for influence and for the scientific approach.

He took up office in April 1895 with a brief which appeared simply to be the conduct of investigations, here and overseas, to show how the English school system might be improved. Taking German education as an obvious point of reference, he immediately started his visits to that country and learned to speak and write the language. Over the next few years a steady flow of reports appeared under his management, full of information brought back from all parts of the world. But the position was a simple one only superficially. As a civil servant required to respond to the demands of the Committee of Council on Education he soon found himself involved in drafting legislation. Acland deplored this over-willing entry into what was becoming a hotly political arena, their long and productive friendship ended, and (it would seem) Acland's willingness to press his interests. Anxious to see his views on education given effect, eager to put his knowledge and perception at the service of his masters, Sadler drifted into a thoroughly false position, where he was at the mercy of the necessary horse-trading and the intrigue and careerism of senior civil servants and politicians. Disappointed in his

hope that he would be given charge of secondary education in the new Board of Education, he finally fell victim to his former assistant, now Permanent Secretary of the Board, Robert Morant. The affairs of the Department and Board in these years, and the enigmatic Morant himself, still absorb the best attentions of historians. Suffice it to say here that in May 1903 Sadler was forced into resignation after a dispute over the scope of his official duties. The affair was conducted in a minor blaze of publicity.

It has been said that Sadler was not ambitious in the ordinary sense, but (true to the Oxford of his youth) believed that he should do his duty to the utmost. He was aware of his own abilities and confident in his highly-developed knowledge; he sensed also that he had an especially valuable awareness of what education was all about. Twice during his time at the Education Department he refused to consider principalships of university colleges, believing presumably that he would have more influence if he remained at the centre of things.

Sadler's activities between 1895 and 1903 laid the foundation of what some of his admirers consider the most significant intellectual achievement of his career — the development of a comparative approach to the study of education more thorough and sophisticated than anything previously attempted in England. At the same time one must recognise that all these enquiries were inspired by an abiding concern to discover the essence of *English* social and public affairs. Already as an undergraduate Sadler had come under the influence of Liberal Idealists who had discovered in the ideas of 'nationality' and 'citizenship' a moral solution to the conflict of individualism and collectivism. 'National life' was an important phrase in his vocabulary and, like his early mentors, he saw education in all its varieties as the formative social institution.

Thus Sadler took the break with the Board of Education very badly, feeling that it had wrecked his chances of influencing the shape of English national life. Still, his repute was such that he was able to step immediately into a part-time professorship of history and administration of education specially set up for him by Manchester University, and he began to work as a free-lance consultant, advising the new local education authorities on the discharge of their responsibilities under the 1902 Act. Another series of reports followed. He was also much exercised about the prospects for further and technical education, an area in which Robert Morant's particular brand of élitism was doing the country

no good at all, and in 1907 the monumental Manchester volume on *Continuation schools in England and elsewhere* appeared under his editorship. Then he became involved in the problems of religious education and found himself advising the Church of England on what could be done about the lingering hostility to denominational schools.

Sadler worked in this way for eight years, but still with the feeling that his career had been stunted. In his biography of his father Michael Sadleir dates the first serious adventures as an art-collector to this period, and interprets the sometimes reckless buying of pictures as a way of warding off depression.

In this middle period of his life he seems to have had more leisure (if that is the right word) to examine the questions of what was fundamental to the English approach to education. Politics had changed since his youth and he moved firmly to the centre; in an undenominational way he became more religious. The answers he now produced to his own questions had always been implicit in his work. The old theme of moral influence appeared as an assertion of the essentially spiritual bed-rock of education. Never unduly impressed by his discoveries in other countries, he believed that the problem for the English was to find a modern balance of the old English dualities of idealism and utility, excellence and equality, local or individual initiative and administrative efficiency.

He was now, in the estimation of many of his contemporaries, the country's foremost authority on education. In 1911 two honours came, when he was made a Companion of the Bath and invited to become Vice-Chancellor of the University of Leeds. His son has suggested that the Leeds post was second-best and that throughout his tenure Michael Sadler nursed the hope that he might be summoned to be administrative head of the country's central authority for education. Leeds was certainly a very different place from the first University whose interests he had sought to further. It had begun as a 'local college' dominated by its industrial and commercial patrons, had been pushed into almost reluctant chartered independence in 1904, and was still small, unimposing and not at all renowned. Nevertheless the new Vice-Chancellor believed that it offered him the best chance of personal happiness and scope to spread light and to encourage the scientific approach to affairs, to serve both learning and the local community.

He saw Leeds through the difficult days of the Great War and then the slump. There were fears at times that the University might not be able to survive, but he did much for its financial standing and reputation. He demanded much of his staff, and also put himself tirelessly at the service of colleagues and students. He made sure that new ventures in adult education succeeded, and by his involvement in so many of the city's cultural and social activities became a one-man external relations committee.

Unfortunately other familiar fates pursued Sadler to Leeds. His idealistic but ill-judged response to the municipal strike of 1913 has entered the history books. The Left was incensed by his official encouragement of students to go strike-breaking, and the labour movement in West Yorkshire remained antipathetic towards the University for a good many years afterwards. He even managed to fall foul of the Right, in their case because of his refusal on grounds of principle to reprimand the dissident members of his own staff who publicly opposed him. He was not uniformly respected by the city's leaders and other uncomfortable incidents followed in later years; one which is still talked about concerned his determination to stand by the University war memorial commissioned from the sculptor Eric Gill and considered by some to be offensive to the ethos of a commercial town. Mishaps of this kind, going back a long time, had already allowed his enemies to spread the myth that he was not a sound administrator; they may indeed have ensured that he was thwarted in his greatest ambition.

There was an absence from Leeds of some eighteen months, from October 1917 to April 1919, when Sadler acted as president of the Calcutta University Commission. He succeeded in widening the inquiry to include a critique of the whole condition of Indian education, and managed to produce a voluminous and high-minded report on higher education in the sub-continent, despite a number of near fatal conflicts among his membership. He had now added to his many qualifications that of being an authority on Indian education, and on his return to England he became Sir Michael Sadler KCSI, Knight Commander of the Star of India.

The final move of a distinguished career came in June 1923 when he returned to his first academic home as Master of University College, Oxford (and soon found himself chairman of the Delegacy for Extra-Mural Studies, successor of the body to which nearly forty years earlier

he had been the first real secretary). He was over sixty; the pace became slower but the old urge to make things happen remained strong. For a time he was busy in the work of organising a badly-needed financial and physical extension to the Bodleian Library, and much of his energy in the last years went into the business of the Oxford Preservation Trust, devoted to finding a *modus vivendi* between an ancient University and a rapidly-growing industrial city.

Sadler resigned his Mastership in September 1934, and for the next several years kept up his wide involvement in the educational affairs of England and the British dominions and colonies. He died on 14 October 1943 at Headington, Oxford.

Michael Sadler's interests, some of them maintained into his eighties, were richer and more numerous than can be indicated in the space available here. They are well described in the biographies written by Michael Sadleir and Lynda Grier, and referred to in Dr Pickering's introductory notes. Those books also offer, in their very different ways, an overall assessment of the man's life and career, another task beyond the scope of this short introduction. To the evidence of those who knew of his doings at first hand is now added this authoritative guide to what principally remains — Sir Michael Sadler's great and varied record of published writing.

The scope of the bibliography

The intention of the bibliography is to provide as complete as possible a listing of Sir Michael Sadler's published writings. The great majority of these are on educational topics, but other subjects (for example, art, the conservation of the environment) become commoner after 1920. One posthumous publication is included, but not items from his unpublished papers printed since his death by other writers.

The term 'published writings' is broadly interpreted to include private publications, and memoranda and other printed ephemera, if written at the request of, or addressed to, an institution or corporate body. Some of the main categories of material included are books, written or edited; essays and articles; lectures and addresses, if printed as self-contained items; letters to the press; published exchanges of correspondence; introductions to other people's work; book reviews; and informal speeches at conferences if printed as part of the official proceedings.

Excluded categories are press reports of speeches; addresses printed in school magazines; interviews; reports of committees of which Sadler was only an ordinary member; and reports and documents written in a purely official capacity (principally as Secretary of the University of Oxford Extension Delegacy and as Vice-Chancellor of the University of Leeds). The decision to exclude press reports of speeches was taken partly for bibliographical reasons, since Sadler was by all accounts one of the great speakers of his day and such reports are very numerous. The thematic content of his principal speeches was, however, usually published in some form or other, and Sadler was a frequent re-user of his own material: consequently it is not very likely that the excluded speeches, though full of interest for their exposition and detail, contain much of major importance not available elsewhere.

The same is probably true of the bulk of the manuscript and type-script speeches among Sadler's unpublished papers, especially now that Dr Higginson has made some of the most significant available in his *Selections*. Much of this material is deposited in the Brotherton Library where it is available to researchers, although it is not yet catalogued or numbered. It was drawn on for the present writer's 'An exhibition of selected publications and writings of Sir Michael Sadler in the field of comparative education', published in *Proceedings of the eleventh annual*

conference of the Comparative Education Society in Europe (British Section) at the University of Leeds, September 17–20th 1976, edited by Colin Brock and Daniel F. McDade (1977), pp. 125–32. The Brotherton's manuscript and typescript holdings also contain, *inter alia*, Sadler's study of his great-great-uncle, 'Michael Thomas Sadler, M.P., F.R.S.: a sketch of his life and opinions' (1896), and a quantity of his unpublished writings on art. The Bodleian Library has Sadler's diaries from 1912 until his death, and a mass of other papers, principally relating to his work for the Board of Education, the Oxford Preservation Trust, and the Bodleian Library itself, but also including a copy of his unfinished 'Comments on the history of education in England'. Dr Higginson has printed extracts from this in his *Selections*, and diary entries have been printed by Michael Sadleir and Lynda Grier in their books on Sadler. Another special collection of Sadler material, including letters, notebooks, and newspaper cuttings, exists in the University Research Library, University of California, Los Angeles.

I have also not included in the bibliography items whose existence I have been unable to verify. In her list of 'Major publications by M. E. Sadler' *(Achievement in education,* pp. ix–xi), Lynda Grier included under 1908 a book entitled 'The English scholarship system', jointly written with H. Bompas Smith and supposedly published by Longmans, but I have found no evidence for its publication. Miss Grier also lists as a self-contained publication a report on Sheffield Training College, 1904, but the College was covered by Sadler's 1903 report for the City of Sheffield Education Committee, and this separate report is likely to be another ghost. In the early 1890s the publisher John Murray was advertising 'Problems of political economy' as forthcoming from Sadler, but this seems never to have appeared. Sadler himself refers to another apparently unpublished book in his letter to *Time and tide* of 6 October 1934: 'Sometime in the 'nineties, stung into new ideas by Sir Halford Mackinder's lectures on geography, I wrote a short book under the title of *The two-mindedness of England'*. Other unfulfilled literary projects are mentioned by Sadleir, pp. 105–06.

Items have also been excluded if I have been unable to trace any details of their publication. Thus I have had to omit several publications listed as by Sadler in *The Department of Education in the University of Manchester, 1890–1911* (see no. 247 in the bibliography), including an April 1910 'The two-mindedness of England'. Other examples are

'Technical, commercial and industrial education in Great Britain and Ireland, 1895', listed under Sadler in Paul Monroe's *Cyclopedia of education*, II (1911), p. 482; a handful of book reviews known to have been printed somewhere; and several seeming publications referred to in passing in the diaries.

The bibliography therefore cannot claim to be 'complete', despite its 631 items, and with a writer like Sir Michael Sadler it is always likely that new items will be identified (for example the contributions to the *Manchester guardian* referred to collectively by Sadler, p. 108). I should consequently be very grateful for information about any publication that I have missed.

Notes on arrangement and presentation

Entries in the bibliography are arranged chronologically by year, and alphabetically by title within each year, except when Sadler made several contributions to the same publication in which case they are grouped together. A title is supplied if one does not not exist, for example [Review of], [Speech at]. The entries are numbered consecutively in a single sequence. Every published item is given a separate entry and number except in the case of Sadler's monthly column 'Education in England' in *Indian education* from 1903–22 (for which a collective entry is provided immediately before the entries for 1903) and his leading articles for the *Morning post* at the time of the debate on the 1906 Education Bill, which are given the single entry no. 143. Cross-references to the original entry are provided in the case of significant later reprintings. Annotations are provided if the title of an item is unhelpful or misleading, and in certain other special cases. An asterisk(*) before an item number indicates that either the original or a copy of the item is available in the Brotherton Library. A subject index follows the bibliography.

Abbreviations

Grier   Lynda Grier, *Achievement in education: the work of Michael Ernest Sadler, 1885–1935* (London: Constable, 1952)

Higginson   J. H. Higginson (compiler), *Selections from Michael Sadler: studies in world citizenship* (Liverpool: Dejall & Meyorre, 1979)

Sadleir   Michael Sadleir, *Michael Ernest Sadler (Sir Michael Sadler, K.C.S.I.), 1861–1943: a memoir by his son* (London: Constable, 1949)

Sir Michael Sadler: a bibliography

1877

*1 'Luther, A.D. 1510' [poem], *T.V.W.*, no. 3 (15 Dec. 1877), p. 43.

The Rugby School magazine. Sadler's contributions are identified in Sadleir, p. 22n (nos. 1–3, 5–7), and in an annotated set of the magazine in Rugby School Library (nos.1–4, 6–7, 9). The above item is signed "E", like the other poems (nos. 4 and 9).

*2 'A walk to Daventry', *T.V.W.*, no. 3 (15 Dec. 1877), pp. 38–40.

Signed "M". Untitled in the issue itself, but as above in the index to 1877–78.

1878

*3 'Bells and belfries', *T.V.W.*, no. 8 (6 June 1878), pp. 130–31.

Signed "M".

*4 'Chess' [poem], *T.V.W.*, no. 12 (14 Nov. 1878), p. 202.

Signed "E".

*5 'The danger of socialism', *T.V.W.*, no. 6 (25 March 1878), pp. 90–92.

Signed "M".

*6 'Faith practical', *T.V.W.*, no. 4 (2 Feb. 1878), pp. 62–65.

Signed "M".

*7 'An old Chartist', *T.V.W.*, no. 9 (3 July 1878), pp. 143–45.

Unsigned.

*8 'A poet's birthplace', *T.V.W.*, no. 11 (12 Oct. 1878), pp. 185–87.

On Tennyson. Not attributed to Sadler either in Sadleir or by the annotator [see note to no. 1 above], bus signed "M". No items in *T.V.W.* other than those by Sadler are signed "M".

*9 'A vision of Cock Houses' [poem], *T.V.W.*, no. 13 (18 Dec. 1878), p. 216.

  Signed "E".

1881

*10 'Rugby School: II, the school life', in *Everyday life in our public schools sketched by head-scholars of Eton, Winchester, Westminster, Shrewsbury, Harrow, Rugby, Charterhouse . . .*, edited by Charles Eyre Pascoe (London: Griffith and Farran, 1881), pp. 178–92.

1883

11 [Review of] Samuel Waddington, *Arthur Hugh Clough: a monograph* (London, 1883), in *Oxford magazine*, 24 Jan. 1883, pp. 18–19.

1885

*12 *Syllabus of a course of lectures on 'Past, present, and future of the working classes, and how to better their condition', with a statement and criticism of the views held by famous political economists, to be given in the New Islington Hall, Ancoats, Manchester, on Monday, Sept. 7th, and each Monday till Nov. 23rd, 1885* (Manchester, [n.d.]). 31 pp.

1887

13 [Answer to remarks about university extension lectures for elementary teachers], in *Oxford University extension lectures: report of a conference . . . of representatives of the local committees . . . and others interested in the extension of university teaching, Apr. 20, 21 1887* (Oxford, 1887), pp. 100–01.

1889

14   *Syllabus of lectures on the economic force of combination, as illustrated by the history of merchant gilds, craft gilds, trades unions, syndicates, productive and distributive co-operation* (Oxford, 1889). 22 pp.

15   *Three lectures on the beginnings of modern socialism, delivered at the summer meeting of university extension students in Oxford, August, 1889* (Oxford, 1889). 67 pp.

1890

*16   'A golden opportunity for university extension', *Paternoster review,* Dec. 1890, pp. 217–26.

Reprinted as a pamphlet with additional prefatory note, 1891.

17   'Note on Oxford extension affairs', *University extension journal,* 1 no. 2 (March 1890), 16.

18   'Note on the Oxford Summer Meeting', *University extension journal,* 1 no. 1 (Feb. 1890), 4.

*19   *University extension: has it a future?* [with H. J. Mackinder] (London: Frowde, 1890). vii, 141 pp.

See also no. 26 below.

1891

20   'A college in every town' [letter], *Oxford University extension gazette,* 1 (1890–91), 84.

Sadler apparently acted as editor of the monthly *Gazette* from its inception in 1890 until 1895 (Grier, p. 15), but is not named as such in the publication itself.

21   'A college in every town', *Oxford University extension gazette*, 2 (1891–92), 2–3.

22   *On the eve of change: suggestions for the future development of university extension teaching* (Oxford, 1891). 11 pp.

23   'The origin of university extension' [letter], *University extension journal*, 1 no. 13 (Feb. 1891), 8.

24   'The prospects of university extension in England', *University extension*, 1 (1891–92), 33–40.

> Reprinted in *Handbook of university extension*, edited by George Francis James, second edition (Philadelphia: American Society for the Extension of University Teaching, 1893), pp. 33–40.

*25 [Review article on W. Sewell, *Suggestion for the extension of the University* (Oxford, 1850), and other works on university extension], in *Quarterly review*, 172 (1891), 399–430.

> Unsigned.

*26 *University extension, past, present, and future* [with H. J. Mackinder] (London: Cassell, 1891). viii, 144 pp.

> "The third edition, revised and enlarged, of 'University extension: has it a future?'" [no. 19 above]. The second edition seems to have been a reprint of the first.

1892

27   'A college of economic science', *Oxford University extension gazette*, 2 (1891–92), 142.

*28 'The development of university extension', in *The proceedings of the first annual meeting of the National Conference on University Extension, held in Philadelphia, December 29–31, 1891, under the auspices of the American Society for the Extension of University Teaching*, compiled by George Francis James (Philadelphia: Lippincott, 1892), pp. 63–82.

Reprinted as a pamphlet (Philadelphia: Lippincott, 1892) as publication 10 of the Society.

The volume also contains:

*29   'The organization and function of local centres', *ibid.*, pp. 113–20.

Reprinted as a pamphlet (Philadelphia: Lippincott, 1892) as publication 12 of the Society.

30   'An "extension" degree', *Oxford University extension gazette*, 3 (1892–93), 9–10.

31   'In reply to M. Espinas', *Oxford University extension gazette*, 2 (1891–92), 128–30.

An extract from Espinas' appreciation of university extension in Great Britain and the United States is printed immediately beforehand.

*32   'Mr Gladstone at Oxford: lecture on the growth and influence of universities', *Manchester guardian*, 25 Oct. 1982, p.5.

"From our special correspondent" (otherwise unsigned). Referred to in Sadleir, p. 117. See also the next item.

*33   'Mr Gladstone's visit to Oxford', *Manchester guardian*, 26 Oct. 1892, p.5.

"From a special correspondent". See the previous item.

*34   *Syllabus of a course of lectures on socialism, past and present, with an outline of a course of study*, University extension lectures, series A, 40 (Philadelphia: American Society for the Extension of University Teaching, 1892). 39 pp.

*35   *Syllabus of a course of lectures on the change in political economy, with an outline of a course of study*, University extension lectures, [series A, 41 (Philadelphia: American Society for the Extension of University Teaching, 1892)]. 26 pp.

Lacks imprint etc., but advertised, with series number, in the preceding item.

*36   'University extension', in *Oxford and Oxford life*, edited by J. Wells (London: Methuen, 1892), pp. 164–90.

37   'Will university extension starve the college staffs?', *University extension*, 1 (1891–92), 369–76.

> Reprinted in *Handbook of university extension* [see no. 24 above], pp. 369–76.

1893

38   'The bearing of the new code of regulations for evening continuation schools on university extension work', *Oxford University extension gazette*, 3 (1892–93), 137.

39   'The extension movement and the county councils', *University extension journal*, 4 no. 41 (Nov. 1893), 23–25.

*40   [Letter from M. E. Sadler to Dr W. Ince relating to a proposal for the summoning of a conference on secondary education by the University of Oxford]. 15 pp.

> Printed "for members of the Hebdomadal Council". Dated at end, April 4, 1893. Reprinted in Higginson, pp. 23–28.

1894

*41   'The facts about university extension', *Nineteenth century*, 36 (1894), 371–82.

> A reply to Charles Whibley, 'The farce of "university extension"', *ibid.*, 203–10.

*42   [Speech in] *Report of the proceedings [of the] University Extension Congress, London, 1894* (London: King, [n.d.]), pp. 45–47.

> Seconding the adoption of a report.

1895

43   'The first experiments in the extension of university teaching', *Oxford University extension gazette*, 5 (1894–95), 109–12.

*44 'On the leaving examination as conducted in the secondary schools of Prussia', in *Report*, [of the] Royal Commission on Secondary Education, C.7862 (London: H.M.S.O., 1895), V, pp. 27–33.

> Reprinted in *Appendix to the first report of the Commissioners,* Intermediate Education (Ireland) Commission, C.9117 (Dublin: H.M.S.O., 1898), pp. 376–78, and in *Essays on examinations* (no. 588 below).
> The *Report* of the Royal Commission on Secondary Education also contains:

*45 'The various methods of securing representation of teachers' [with Sophie Bryant], *ibid.*, pp. 20–26.

1896

46 'The testimonial to Mr. Sadler' [letter], *University extension journal*, new series, 1 (1896), 135.

47 'University extension: l'extension des universités en Angleterre', in *L'éducation populaire des adultes en Angleterre: notices sur les principales institutions par des membres de leurs comités; avec une préface de F. Buisson* (Paris: Hachette, 1896), pp. 45–83.

1897

48 'By the test of facts: an episode in the life of Pestalozzi', *University extension journal*, new series, 2 (1897), 51–52.

*49 'Michael Ferrebee Sadler', in *Dictionary of national biography*, 50 (1897), p. 105.

*50 'Michael Thomas Sadler', in *Dictionary of national biography*, 50 (1897), pp. 105–09.

51 'Movements in English education: denominational teaching', *Citizen* [Philadelphia?], August 1897, pp. 132–34.

Signed "X". This and nos. 52–54 are identified as by Sadler in copies in the Department of Education and Science Library, London.

52 'Movements in English education: home and school', *Citizen*, March 1897, pp. 9–12.

Signed "X".

53 'Movements in English education: the teachers' societies', *Citizen*, June 1897, pp. 85–87.

Signed "X".

54 'Some current topics in English schools: the training of young children', *Citizen*, Feb. 1897, pp. 401–02.

Signed "X".

*55 *Special reports on educational subjects, 1896–7* [editor; prepared by the Office of Special Inquiries and Reports of the] Education Department, C.8447 (London: H.M.S.O., 1897). iv, 732 pp.

Sadler contributed an introductory letter and the following papers:

*56 'The admission of women to universities: summary of the arrangements in force at the chief universities in the British Empire and abroad' [with J. W. Longsdon], *ibid.*, pp. 689–719.

*57 'A brief sketch of the history of the Irish system of elementary education (with a table of dates showing the reciprocal influence of Irish on English, and of English on Irish, education)', *ibid.*, pp. 211–40.

*58 'List of the chief official papers on education in Great Britain and Ireland', *ibid.*, pp. 720–31 (appendix).

*59 'The Oberrealschulen of Prussia, with special reference to the Oberrealschule at Charlottenburg', *ibid.*, pp. 435–69.

*60 'Public elementary education in England and Wales, 1870–1895' [with J. W. Edwards], *ibid.*, pp. 1–71.

*61   'Recent legislation on elementary education in Belgium' [with R. L. Morant], *ibid.*, pp. 258–72.

*62   'The Realschulen in Berlin, and their bearing on questions of secondary and commercial education', *ibid.*, pp. 375–434.

1898

*63   'A correction' [letter], *Journal of Education*, n.s. 20 (1898), 276.

A correction to the report in an earlier issue (*ibid.*, p. 251) of a lecture of his on school curricula.

*64   'Memorandum on manual training for boys in primary schools in foreign countries', in *Appendices to the reports of the Commissioners, Commission on Manual and Practical Instruction in Primary Schools under the Board of National Education in Ireland*, C.8925 (Dublin: H.M.S.O., 1898), pp. 15–26 (appendix A.V).

*65   *Special reports on educational subjects*, II [editor; prepared by the Office of Special Inquiries and Reports of the] Education Department, C.8943 (London: H.M.S.O., 1898). vii, 694 pp.

Sadler contributed an introductory letter and the following paper:

*66   'Summary of statistics, regulations, etc. of elementary education in England and Wales, 1833–1870' [with J. W. Edwards], *ibid.*, pp. 434–544.

*67   *Special reports on educational subjects*, III [editor; prepared by the Office of Special Inquiries and Reports of the] Education Department, C.8988 (London: H.M.S.O., 1898). vi, 697 pp.

Sadler contributed an introductory letter and the following papers:

*68   'Higher commercial education in Antwerp, Leipzig, Paris, and Havre', *ibid.*, pp. 554–626.

9

*69   'Problems in Prussian secondary education for boys, with special reference to similar questions in England', *ibid.*, pp. 83–252.

Reprinted as 'Special reports on secondary education in Prussia, 1.'

1899

*70   'Address', *Practical teacher*, 20 (1899), 282–84.

Given at a meeting of the National Home-Reading Union.

*71   'Memorandum on the inspection and examination of secondary schools', in *Appendix to the final report of the Commissioners, Part II: miscellaneous documents*, Intermediate Education (Ireland) Commission, C.9513 (Dublin: H.M.S.O., 1899), pp. 285–90.

Reprinted in *Educational review*, 21 (1900), 497–515.

*72   *Secondary education in its bearings on practical life: an address delivered at Howick, Northumberland, on August 26th, 1899* (Newcastle-on-Tyne: Ward, 1899). 23 pp.

Reprinted in Higginson, pp. 28–35.

1900

73   *Des sciences sociales dans les écoles secondaires anglaises* (Paris: Alcan, 1900). 20 pp.

A paper given at the "Congrès international de l'enseignement des sciences sociales, Paris, 30 Juillet–3 Août 1900".

*74   *How far can we learn anything of practical value from the study of foreign systems of education? Notes of an address given at the Guildford Educational Conference, on Saturday, October 20, 1900* (Guildford, 1900). 19 pp.

Reprinted in Higginson, pp. 48–51.

*75   'Impending changes in national education', *Manchester guardian*,
      21 Feb. 1900, p. 12.
      An unsigned review of the Hon. E. Lyulph Stanley, *Our national
      education* (London, 1899).

*76   'In what sense ought schools to prepare boys and girls for life?',
      Saint George: the journal of the Ruskin Society of Birmingham, 3
      (1900), 97–113.
      Reprinted in Higginson, pp. 35–40.

*77   *Special reports on educational subjects, VI: Preparatory schools
      for boys: their place in English secondary education* [editor;
      prepared by the Office of Special Inquiries and Reports of the]
      Board of Education, Cd.418 (London: H.M.S.O., 1900). xxxi,
      834 pp.
      Sadler contributed an introductory letter and the following paper:

*78   'The place of the preparatory school for boys in secondary educa-
      tion in England', *ibid.*, pp. 79–90.

1901

79   'England's need of commercial education', in *The King's Weigh
      House lectures to business men* (London: Macmillan, 1901),
      pp. 9–40.

*80   'National education and social ideals', in *Education in the nine-
      teenth century: lectures delivered in the Education Section of the
      Cambridge University Extension Summer Meeting in August
      1900*, edited by R. D. Roberts (Cambridge: Cambridge University
      Press, 1901), pp. 210–39.

*81   *Special reports on educational subjects, IV: Educational systems
      of the chief colonies of the British Empire (Dominion of Canada,
      Newfoundland, West Indies)* [editor; prepared by the Office of
      Special Inquiries and Reports of the] Board of Education, Cd.416
      (London: H.M.S.O., 1901). xxv, 838 pp.
      Sadler contributed an introductory letter and the following papers:

*82 'Note on the Macdonald Manual Training Fund for the development of manual and practical instruction in primary schools in Canada', *ibid.*, pp. 537–40.

*83 'The system of education in Jamaica' [with the Hon. T. Capper], *ibid.*, pp. 575–749.

> Reprinted as 'Special reports on the systems of education in the West Indies, and in British Guiana, 1'.

*84 'The teaching of agriculture in elementary and higher schools in the West Indies', *ibid.*, pp. 797–834.

> Reprinted as 'Special reports on the systems of education in the West Indies, and in British Guiana, 3'.

*85 *Special reports on educational subjects, V: Educational systems of the chief colonies of the British Empire* (*Cape Colony, Natal, Commonwealth of Australia, New Zealand, Ceylon, Malta*) [editor; prepared by the Office of Special Inquiries and Reports of the] Board of Education, Cd.417 (London: H.M.S.O., 1901). xv, 532 pp.

> Sadler contributed an introductory letter and the following papers:

*86 'The history and present state of education in Cape Colony' [with G. B. Muir], *ibid.*, pp. 1–195.

> Reprinted as 'Special reports on the systems of education in Cape Colony and Natal, 1'.

*87 'The system of education in New Zealand', *ibid.*, pp. 625–766.

> Reprinted as 'Special report on the system of education in New Zealand'.

*88 *The two-mindedness of England: an address delivered at Reading College, Oct. 2nd, 1901, at the opening of the session, 1901–2* (Reading, [n.d.]). 24 pp.

> Reprinted in *Lectures on empire delivered at 7, Carlton Gardens, 1906–7* [with others, no imprint], pp. 1–9.

1902

*89   'Aims in education', *Present-day papers*, 5 (1902), 72–78.
      Reprinted in Higginson, pp. 60–61.

*90   'Les changements dans le "Board of Education" en Angleterre'
      [letters], *Revue internationale de l'enseignement*, 44 (1902),
      197–98.

91   'The English ideal of education', *Independent* [New York], 54
      (1902), 2015–17.

*92   *Lantern lectures on the British Empire.* 8 pp.
      Memorandum "printed for the use of the Colonial Office (Miscellane-
      ous no. 150)". Dated December 1902.

*93   *Plan for imperial education.* 4 pp.
      Unsigned. "Accompanying a letter from the Education Committee of
      the Victoria League [to the Rhodes Trustees], dated November 27th,
      1902". See no. 104 below.

94   'Points of contrast in the educational situation in England and in
      America', *Educational review*, 24 (1902), 217–27.

*95   *Special reports on educational subjects*, VII: *Rural education in
      France* [editor: prepared by the Office of Special Inquiries and
      Reports of the] Board of Education, Cd.834 (London: H.M.S.O.,
      1902). xiv, 318 pp.
      Sadler contributed an introductory letter.

*96   *Special reports on educational subjects*, VIII: *Education in Scan-
      dinavia, Switzerland, Holland, Hungary, etc., with a supplement,
      Education in the Netherlands* [editor; prepared by the Office of
      Special Inquiries and Reports of the] Board of Education, Cd.835,
      1157, 2 vols (London: H.M.S.O., 1902). vii, 703 + iii, 83 pp.
      Sadler contributed an introductory letter and the following paper:

*97   'Note on children's workshops in Sweden' [with J. G. Legge],
      ibid., pp. 143–47.

*98   *Special reports on educational subjects, IX: Education in Germany*
       [editor; prepared by the Office of Special Inquiries and Reports of
       the] Board of Education, Cd.836 (London: H.M.S.O., 1902). xiv,
       622 pp.

       Sadler contributed an introductory letter and the following papers:

*99   'Recent developments in higher commercial education in Ger-
       many', *ibid.*, pp. 487–525.

*100   'The unrest in secondary education in Germany and elsewhere',
       ibid., pp. vii–xiv, 1–191.

*101   *Special reports on educational subjects, X–XI: Education in the
       United States of America* [editor; prepared by the Office of Special
       Inquiries and Reports of the] Board of Education, Cd.837, 1156,
       2 vols (London: H.M.S.O., 1902). vi, 538 + v, 624 pp.

       Sadler contributed an introductory letter and the following papers:

*102   'A contrast between German and American ideals in education',
       ibid., pp. 433–70.

*103   'The education of the coloured race', *ibid.*, pp. 521–60.

*104   *Visual instruction by lantern slides.* 7 pp.

       Memorandum, explicitly by Sadler, forming an appendix to no. 93
       above. Reprinted in Higginson, pp. 58–59.

1903-22

105   'Education in England', *Indian education: a monthly record*
       (1903–22).

       A monthly article in each issue from vol. 1, no. 9 (April 1903) to vol. 20,
       no. 12 (July 1922) — when *Indian education* ceased publication — with
       the exception of vol. 14, no. 7 (Feb. 1916), vol. 16, nos. 5, 7–12 (Dec.
       1917, Feb.–July 1918), and the whole of vol. 17 (August 1918–July
       1919). The first five articles, in vol. 1, nos. 9–12, and vol. 2, no. 1, are
       signed "Oxoniensis".

The Sept. 1911 article was reprinted in *Educational times* of 1 Feb. 1912 (no. 256 below), and the March 1915 article in *Secondary education* of Sept. 1915 (no. 301 below). In addition, the article for November 1917, with the sub-title 'Parallel movements in German and English education since the beginning of the war', is reprinted in Higginson, pp. 117–20. Extracts from the articles of Sept. 1912, Sept. 1919, Oct. 1919, Jan. 1920, August 1920 and Oct. 1920 are also reprinted in Higginson, pp. 124–32. See also no. 118 below.

1903

106 'Applied science and social control', *Saint George*, 6 (1903), 277–86.

*107 'Emerson's influence in education', *Journal of education*, n.s. 25 (1903), 669–71.

Reprinted in *Educational review*, 26 (1903), 457–63.

*108 'The ferment in education on the continent and in America', *Proceedings of the British Academy*, 1 (1903), 81–94.

*109 'Impressions of American education', *Educational news*, 10 Jan. 1903, pp. 39–42.

Reprinted in *Educational review*, 25 (1903), 217–31; in *A history of international and comparative education: nineteenth-century documents*, [edited by] Stewart E. Fraser [and] William W. Brickman (Glenview, Ill.: Scott, Foresman, 1968), pp. 474–80; and in Higginson, pp. 53–57.

*110 'Individuality in education and the claims of the state', *Child life*, 5 (1903), 57–61.

*111 'Introduction', pp. xi–xiv, to *Co-education: a series of essays by various authors*, edited by Alice Woods (London: Longmans, Green, 1903).

*112 'Mr. Sadler's resignation' [letter], *The Times*, 14 July 1903, p.10.

15

*113　*National ideals in education: an inaugural lecture, delivered for the session 1903–4, at the University College of Wales, Aberystwyth, Thursday, October 23rd, 1903* (Aberystwyth, [n.d.]). iii, 18 pp.

Reprinted in *The study of education: a collection of inaugural lectures*, edited by Peter Gordon (London: Woburn Press, 1980), I, pp. 54–75.

*114　'The new education committees' [letter], *The Times*, 22 Jan. 1903, p. 5.

Signed "Sigma".

*115　*Papers relating to the resignation of the Director of Special Inquiries and Reports*, Board of Education, Cd.1602 (London: H.M.S.O., 1903). 70 pp.

Includes numerous minutes, letters, and other documents by Sadler.

*116　*Report on secondary and higher education [in Sheffield]* (London: Eyre & Spottiswoode, [for] City of Sheffield Education Committee, 1903). 45 pp.

An abridgement of the report is printed in *The record of technical and secondary education*, 12 (1903), 427–56.

*117　'The Special Inquiries Office at the Board of Education' [letter], *The Times*, 16 May 1903, p. 10.

*118　'The two currents in the new educational movement', *Indian education: a monthly record*, 1 (1903), 546–48.

Separate from the monthly 'Education in England' articles (no. 105 above).

1904

*119　'The fading influence of "laissez-faire"', *Journal of education*, n.s. 26 (1904), 80–82.

On state control in English education.

*120   'Influence of Mr Herbert Spencer's educational writings', *Journal of education*, n.s. 26 (1904), 131–33.

> Reprinted in *Indian journal of education*, 12 (1904), 80–85.

*121   'On school curricula', in *Report of the seventy-third meeting of the British Association for the Advancement of Science, held at Southport in September 1903* (London: Murray, 1904), pp. 876–78.

122   *Report on secondary & technical education in Huddersfield* (London: Eyre & Spottiswoode, [for the] Education Committee of the County Borough of Huddersfield, 1904). 128 pp.

*123   *Report on secondary education in Birkenhead, with chapters on the evening schools and technical classes, and on the training of teachers* (London: Philip, [for the] County-Borough of Birkenhead Education Committee, 1904). 131 pp.

*124   *Report on secondary education in Liverpool: including the training of teachers for public elementary schools* (London: Eyre and Spottiswoode, [for the] City of Liverpool Education Committee, [1904]). [v], iii, 230 pp.

> For the date, see *Journal of education*, n.s. 26 (1904), 748.

*125   'The school in its relation to social organization and to national life', *Educational review*, 28 (1904), 361–77.

> Also printed in [The proceedings of the] *Congress of Arts and Science, Universal Exposition, St. Louis, 1904*, edited by Howard J. Rogers, VIII (Boston: Houghton, Mifflin, 1907), pp. 89–101. Reprinted in Higginson, pp. 62–64.

1905

*126   [Contribution to discussion on] 'Government aid to Friends' schools', *Friends' quarterly examiner*, 39 (1905), 371–78.

*127   'Le grec à Oxford et à Cambridge' [letter], *Revue internationale de l'enseignement*, 49 (1905), 484–86.

*128 'Prof. Sadler's Hampshire report' [letter], *Journal of education,* n.s. 27 (1905), 591–92.

> In reply to a letter in an earlier issue of the *Journal* (pp. 552–53) concerning the Girls' Collegiate School, Aldershot.

129 *Report on secondary & higher education in Derbyshire* (Administrative County of Derby, Education Committee, 1905). iv, 192 pp.

130 *Report on secondary and higher education in Exeter* (Exeter: City and County of Exeter Education Committee, 1905). 71 pp.

131 *Report on secondary & higher education in Hampshire* (Portsmouth: County Council of the County of Southampton, [1905]). 154 pp.

> For the date, see *Journal of education,* n.s. 27 (1905), 457.

*132 *Report on secondary and higher education in Newcastle-upon-Tyne* (Newcastle-upon-Tyne: Newcastle-upon-Tyne Education Committee, 1905). 88 pp.

*133 'The school in some of its relations to social organisation and to national life', *Sociological papers,* 2 (1905), 123–31.

> "Abstract of a paper read before the Sociological Society". Followed by discussion, and then by 'Professor Sadler's reply', pp. 138–39. A shortened version is printed in *Educational review,* 29 (1905), 338–41.

134 *A visit to a school doing a new work.* 16 pp.

> Brunswick Street School, Manchester. For the date, see *Journal of education,* n.s. 27 (1905), 458.

1906

*135 'Denominational schools in English education' [letter], *The Times,* 25 Jan. 1906, p. 11.

*136 'Dr W. T. Harris' [letter], *Journal of education,* 28 (1906), 744–45.

*137 'Drifting towards secularism: a national danger', *Morning post*, 19 Nov. 1906, p. 7.

*138 'French influences in English education', *Modern language teaching*, 2 (1906), 161–70.
Reprinted in *Educational review*, 33 (1907), 145–61, and in Higginson, pp. 65–70. A French version, 'L'influence française sur l'éducation anglaise', was printed in *Revue internationale de l'enseignement*, 52 (1906), 26–40.

139 'The future of denominational schools', *Independent review*, 9 (1906), 253–63.

*140 'Head mistresses for co-educational secondary schools' [letter], *Journal of education*, 28 (1906), 24.

*141 'The House of Lords and the Education Bill' [letter], *Morning post*, 22 Oct. 1906, p. 7.
Reprinted in *Educational review*, 32 (1906), 536–38.

*142 'In memoriam Richard Claverhouse Jebb', *Revue internationale de l'enseignment*, 51 (1906), 139–42.

*143 [Leading articles on the House of Lords debate on the 1906 Education Bill], *Morning post*, 29 Oct., 31 Oct., 1–3 Nov., 6–9 Nov., 12–13 Nov., 16 Nov., 21 Nov., and 23 Nov. 1906.
Unsigned.

*144 'The national need for higher commercial education', *Journal [of the] Department of Agriculture and Technical Instruction for Ireland*, 6 (1905–06), 233–47.

*145 'The new Education Bill in England', *Educational review*, 32 (1906), 109–31.

*146 'Le nouveau ministre de l'education pour l'Angleterre et le Pays de Galles', *Revue internationale de l'enseignement*, 51 (1906), 61–62.
Signed "M.S." On Augustine Birrell.

*147 'Preface', pp. v–xiii, to *The German universities and university study,* by Friedrich Paulsen; authorized translation by Frank Thilly and William W. Elwang (London: Longmans, Green, 1906).

*148 *Report on secondary and higher education in Essex* (Chelmsford: Essex Education Committee, 1906). v, 418, liv pp.

*149 'Science in national education', in *Science in public affairs,* edited by J. E. Hand (London: Allen, 1906), pp. 75–128.

*150 *A university for Bristol: address delivered at the distribution of prizes for the fiftieth session, 1905–6, [at the] Merchant Adventurers' Technical College, Bristol, on Thursday, December 20th, 1906* (Bristol, [n.d.]). 23 pp.

1907

*151 *A bureau of education for the British Empire: the scope of its work and the possibility of its organisation* (London: Longmans, Green, 1907). 19 pp.

*152 *Continuation schools in England & elsewhere: their place in the educational system of an industrial and commercial state* [editor], University of Manchester publications, 29, Educational series, 1 (Manchester: Manchester University Press, 1907). xxvi, 779 pp.
     "Second edition", 1908.
     Sadler contributed an introduction and the following papers:

*153 'Certain trade schools and pre-apprenticeship schools in England: a brief review of their aims and courses of study' [with Mary S. Beard], *ibid.,* pp. 427–53.

*154 'Compulsory attendance at continuation schools in Germany', *ibid.,* pp. 513–34.

*155   'English employers and the education of their work-people' [with Mary S. Beard], *ibid.*, pp. 265–317.

*156   'Historical review of certain agencies for further education in England', *ibid.*, pp. 1–104.

*157   'The organization of continuation schools in Scotland', *ibid.*, pp. 472–82.

*158   'The present position of state-aided evening schools and classes in England and Wales', *ibid.*, pp. 105–28.

*159   'Should attendance at continuation schools be made compulsory in England?', *ibid.*, pp. 689–749.

*160   'The trend towards industrial training in continuation schools in New England', *ibid.*, pp. 657–73.

*161   'The work of continuation schools in certain rural districts of England' [with Mary S. Beard], *ibid.*, pp. 211–37.

162   'The educational awakening in England', in *Fiftieth anniversary volume, 1857–1906,* [of the] National Education Association of America (Winona, Minn., 1907), pp. 361–66.

*163   'The English scholarship system: its principles and results' [with H. Bompas Smith], *School world,* 9 (1907), 321–23.
       Practically the same as no. 179 below.

*164   'The influence of the state in English education', *Church quarterly review,* 65 (1907–08), 166–92.

*165   'The influence of the state in English education' [letter], *Journal of education,* 29 (1907), 864–66.

*166 *John Ruskin's plan for national education: a lecture ... delivered in St. Margaret's Hall, Dunfermline on November 2, 1907 under the joint auspices of the Carnegie Dunfermline Trust and the School Board of the Burgh of Dunfermline* (Dunfermline, [n.d.]). 31 pp.

   Reprinted in Higginson, pp. 70–76.

*167 'Memorial to the founder of the Art for Schools Association' [letter, with others], *Journal of education*, 29 (1907), 387.

   On the late Miss Mary Elizabeth Christie.

 168 'Nationale Erziehung in England', in *Deutsche Schulerziehung*, herausgegeben von W. Rein (München: Lehmann, 1907), II, 544–67.

*169 'The new work at Sibford School', *Friends' quarterly examiner*, 41 (1907), 427–40.

*170 'Owen, Lovett, Maurice, and Toynbee: their work for adult education in England', *University review*, 5 (1907), 257–66.

   Reprinted in Higginson, pp. 76–79.

*171 'Preface', pp. v–vi, to *Lessons in practical hygiene for use in schools*, by Alice Ravenhill (Leeds: Arnold, 1907).

*172 [Presidential address to Section L, Educational Science], in *Report of the seventy-sixth meeting of the British Association for the Advancement of Science, York, August, 1906* (London: Murray, 1907), pp. 764–76.

  † 'The school in its relation to social organization and to national life'.

   See no. 125 above.

*173 'Science and the Public' [letter], *The Times*, 4 Dec. 1907, p. 10.

*174   Should attendance at continuation schools be made compulsory in England? An address delivered at the Educational Committees' Association Conference . . . Manchester, on Saturday, March 2nd, 1907 (Manchester: Co-operative Wholesale Society Limited, 1907). 14 pp.

*175   'The state and secondary education' [letter], The Times, 24 Dec. 1907. p. 5.

*176   'The state and secondary education' [letter], The Times, 28 Dec. 1907, p. 9.

1908

*177   'After-care generally', in The official report of the Church Congress held at Manchester on October 6th, 7th, 8th and 9th, 1908 (London: Bemrose, 1908), pp. 119–27.

Read at a session entitled 'Care of the Church for her members between the ages of 14 and 21'. Reprinted in Higginson, pp. 82–84.

*178   'Angleterre', in Nouveau dictionnaire de pédagogie et d'instruction primaire, publié sous la direction de F. Buisson (Paris: Hachette, 1908), pp. 61–78.

The Dictionnaire was reprinted in 1911.

*179   'The English scholarship system: its principles and results' [with H. Bompas Smith], in Report of the seventy-seventh meeting of the British Association for the Advancement of Science, Leicester, 31 July – 7 August 1907 (London: Murray, 1908), pp. 707–09.

Practically the same as no. 163 above.

180   'Handwork in history teaching', Educational handwork, 1 (1908), 20–24.

*181 'Handwork in history teaching to children under fourteen years of age' [with others], in *The demonstration schools record, being contributions to the study of education by the Department of Education in the University of Manchester*, edited by J. J. Findlay, I, Publications of the University of Manchester, 32, Education series, 2 (Manchester: University Press, 1908), pp. 94–109.

*182 [Letter on state grants to denominational schools, with T. Edmund Harvey], *The Times*, 4 Dec. 1908, p. 11.

*183 'Moral Education Congress' [letter, with others], *The Times*, 22 August 1908, p. 7.

*184 *Moral instruction and training in schools: report of an international inquiry* [editor], 2 vols (London: Longmans, Green, 1908). lviii, 538 + xxvii, 378 pp.

> Vol. I: The United Kingdom; Vol. II: Foreign and colonial: France, Belgium, Scandinavia, Switzerland, Germany, United States, Canada, Australia, New Zealand and Japan. Sadler provides an 'Introduction', Vol. I, pp. xiii–xlix, and a 'Preface', Vol. II, pp. v–ix, and assists in translating the first chapter.

*185 'Mr McKenna and national education' [letter], *The Times,* 30 Jan. 1908, p. 4.

*186 *Organisations for adult education: their service to English national life: an address to the 69th annual conference of the Lancashire and Cheshire Union of Institutes, at Bootle, Oct. 8th, 1908.* 8 pp.

*187 'Presidential address', in *Papers on moral education communicated to the first International Moral Education Congress held at the University of London. September 25–29, 1908*, edited by C. Spiller (London: Nutt, for the Congress Executive Committee, 1908), pp. 1–6.

> See also *Report of the proceedings of the first International Moral Education Congress* ... (London: Nutt, 1908), pp. 16–17, for Sadler's introductory remarks before his presidential address.

*188 [Presidential address to the North of England Education Con-
ference, Sheffield, January 1908], *School government chronicle*,
79 (1908), 37–38.

*189 'Les projets de lois sur l'enseignement au Parlement du Royaume
Uni en Mai 1908', *Revue internationale de l'enseignement*, 55
(1908), 481–98.

*190 'Should secondary teachers be civil servants?', *A.M.A.: the journal
of the Incorporated Association of Assistant Masters in Secondary Schools*, 3 (1908), 4–7.

Reprinted in Higginson, pp. 85–88.

*191 'Woman suffragists and the House of Commons' [letter], *The
Times*, 12 Oct. 1908, p. 7.

1909

*192 'The International Congress on Moral Education', *International
journal of ethics*, 19 (1908–09), 158–72.

*193 'Introduction', pp. xv–xxxvi, to *Broad lines in science teaching*,
edited by F. Hodson (London: Christophers, [1909]).

Preface dated 1909. Also issued, New York: Macmillan, 1910.
"Second edition", London, 1911.

*194 [Letter on the University of Manchester], *Revue internationale
de l'enseignement*, 57 (1909), 540–42.

Headed "Lettre de M. Sadler, professeur à l'Université de Manchester"

*195 *The present trend of educational thought in England: presidential
address delivered to the [Fulham Educational] Council on October
25th 1909* (Fulham, [n.d.]). 8 pp.

196 'The significance of industrial missions', *East and the West*, 7
(1909), 53–65.

*197   'Teachers and the religious lesson' [letter], *Journal of education*, n.s. 31 (1909), 821.

*198   'Teachers and the religious lesson: the presidential address to the Teachers' Guild, 1909', *Teachers' Guild quarterly*, 33 (1909), 13–38.

1910

*199   'The Census and blind-alley employments during adolescence' [letter], *The Times*, 6 Jan. 1910, p. 11.

*200   [Correspondence with Rev. J. H. Green concerning religious education in schools.] 15 pp.

> "This correspondence is printed by the desire of the Standing Committee of the Voluntary Schools Association in the Diocese of Peterborough". It particularly concerns *Towards educational peace*, no. 216 below. The letters cover the period Sept.–Nov. 1910.

*201   'The educational outlook', *Times educational supplement*, 6 Sept. 1910, pp. 1–2.

> Unsigned.

202   'Geschichte der Erziehung in England und Wales von 1688–1870', in *Encyklopädisches Handbuch der Pädagogik*, herausgegeben von W. Rein, zweite Auflage, X (Langensalza: Beyer, 1910), pp. 686–98.

*203   'High churchmen and the crisis in English education', *Contemporary review*, 98 (1910), 257–72.

*204   *The increase of the powers of the state and of the local authorities in English education, 1850–1910: rapport.* 14 pp.

> A paper given at the Premier Congrès international des sciences administratives, Brussels, 1910. Printed in vol. I of the collected *Rapports* of the Congress (Brussels, 1910), and reprinted in a selection of papers from the Congress, *Problems of local government*, [edited] by G. Montagu Harris (London: King, 1911), pp. 335–47.

*205 'The influence of the late Dr W. T. Harris in English education' [letter], *Journal of education*, n.s. 32 (1910), 78–80.

*206 'Introduction', pp. ix–xi, to *The faith and modern thought: six lectures*, by William Temple (London: Macmillan, 1910).

*207 'Introduction', pp. xi–xiv, to *The training of teachers in England and Wales*, by Peter Sandiford, Contributions to education, 32 (New York: Teachers College, Columbia University, 1910).

   Reprinted in Higginson, pp. 88–89.

*208 *Ladybarn House School, Withington, Manchester: report of the inspector* (1910). 12 pp.

*209 'The new headmaster of Repton' [letter], *Journal of education*, n.s. 32 (1910), 584, 586.

   William Temple.

 210 'The new headmaster of Repton' [letter], *School world*, 12 (1910), 359.

*211 'A proposal for educational peace', *The Times*, 30 May 1910, p. 10.

*212 'The relation of elementary schools to technical schools — day and evening', *School government chronicle*, 83 (1910), 58–61.

   A shortened version is printed as 'Education during adolescence', in *Nature*, 13 Jan. 1910, pp. 325–27.

*213 'The service of William Torrey Harris to British education', *Educational review*, 39 (1910), 191–94.

*214 'Street trading and woman suffrage' [letter], *The Times*, 15 July 1910, p. 8.

 215 'A Surrey school', *Morning post*, 22 July 1910, p. 5.

*216   *Towards educational peace: a plan of re-settlement in English elementary education* [with others]; issued by the Executive Committee of the Educational Settlement Committee (London: Longmans, Green, 1910). 59 pp.

> Sadler was one of the two secretaries of the Committee. He is not credited here with any special responsibility for the publication, but was closely associated with it.

1911

*217   'Acland, Sir Thomas Dyke', in *A cyclopedia of education*, edited by Paul Monroe, I (New York: Macmillan, 1911), pp. 28–29.

> Sadler also contributed the following:

*218   'Arnold, Matthew', *ibid.*, pp. 219–20.

*219   'Arnold, Thomas', *ibid.*, pp. 220–23.

*220   'Baines, Edward', *ibid.*, pp. 318–19.

*221   'Bentham, Jeremy', *ibid.*, pp. 363–64.

*222   'Birkbeck, George', *ibid.*, pp. 384–85.

*223   'Bray, Thomas', *ibid.*, pp. 440–41.

*224   'Brougham, Henry, Baron Brougham and Vaux', *ibid.*, pp. 453–54.

*225   'Brown, John', *ibid.*, pp. 454–55.

*226   *Address . . . delivered at the re-union of old students on the occasion of the jubilee of Stockwell College, June 3rd, 1911.* 4 pp.

> At head of title-page: "British and Foreign School Society".

*227   'Education according to Tolstoy', *Journal of education*, n.s. 33 (1911), 212–14.

> Reprinted in *Educational review*, 41 (1911), 433–40.

*228 'The education of the future', *British congregationalist*, 8 June 1911, p. 484.

> A speech made at the National Conference on the Prevention of Destitution, June 2nd. See also no. 240 below.

229 'Educational peace' [letter], *Guardian*, 30 Jan. 1911, p. 14.

*230 'Ellis, William', in *A cyclopedia of education*, edited by Paul Monroe, II (New York: Macmillan, 1911), pp. 433–35.

> Sadler also contributed the following:

*231 'Endowed Schools Act 1869', *ibid.*, pp. 451–52.

*232 'Fitch, Sir Joshua Girling', *ibid.*, pp. 617–18.

*233 'Forster, William Edward', *ibid.*, pp. 648–50.

*234 'Examinations' [letter], *Times educational supplement*, 7 Feb. 1911, p. 55.

† 'The increase of the powers of the state and of the local authorities in English education (1850–1910)'.

> See no. 204 above.

235 'Introduction', pp. ix–xii, to *The student's Froebel, adapted from Die Menschenerziehung of F. Froebel, by* William H. Herford; revised and edited by D.B. and C.H. . . . 2 vols (London: Pitman, 1911–15).

236 'Introduction', p.v, to *Suggestions for a syllabus in religious teaching,* by G. B. Ayre (London: Longmans, 1911).

237 'Is there a necessary connection between religion and morality?', in *Report of the conference of the World's Student Christian Federation, Robert College, Constantinople, April 24–28, 1911* (World's Student Christian Federation, 1911), pp. 37–39.

*238   'Moral instruction and training in schools', in *The teacher's
        encyclopaedia of the theory, method, practice, history, and
        development of education at home and abroad* . . ., edited by
        A. P. Laurie, I (London: Caxton, 1911), pp. 35–50.

*239   *Pictures in a great city: a paper read at a special meeting of the
        Governors of the Royal Manchester Institution on Thursday,
        March 16, 1911* (Manchester, [n.d.]). 20 pp.

        Reprinted in Higginson, pp. 210–12.

*240   'The presidential address', in *National Conference on the Preven-
        tion of Destitution, held at the Caxton Hall, Westminster, on May
        30th and 31st, and June 1st and 2nd, 1911: report of the proceed-
        ings of the Education Section* (London: King, 1911), pp. 53–57.

        For the speech by Sadler reported on pp. 227–28, see item 228 above.

*241   *The religious question in public education: a critical examination
        of schemes representing various points of view* [with Athelstan
        Riley and Cyril Jackson] (London: Longmans, Green, 1911). vi,
        350 pp.

242   'Schools and scholars: an educational stock-taking', *Morning post*,
        27 Jan. 1911, p. 5.

*243   'The state and English education', *Sociological review*, 4 (1911),
        89–97.

*244   'Suffragists and the Census' [letter], *The Times*, 14 Feb. 1911,
        p. 10.

*245   'Syllabus of a course on the history of education in England,
        1800–1911', in *Outlines of education courses in Manchester Univ-
        ersity,* University of Manchester publications, 61, Educational
        series, 5 (Manchester: University Press, 1911), pp. 1–111.

*246   'The universities, the public schools, and the working class'
        [letter], *Nation*, 12 August 1911, pp. 708–09.

*247 'University day training colleges: their origin, growth, and influence in English education', in *The Department of Education in the University of Manchester, 1890–1911*, University of Manchester publications, 58, Educational series, 4 (Manchester: University Press, 1911), pp. 9–54.

*248 'Zedelijke opvoeding en het 2e Internationaal Congres in 1912 te 'S-Gravenhage te houden', *Geschriften van den Bond ter Behartiging van de Belangen van het Kind*, 2 (1911), 3–21.

On the forthcoming second International Congress on Moral Education, 1912. See no. 264 below.

1912

*249 [Contribution to discussion on representation of teachers and graduates on the governing body of a university], in *Congress of the Universities of the Empire, 1912: report of proceedings*, edited by Alex Hill (London: University of London Press, for the Congress, 1912), pp. 364–65.

*250 'Devonshire fishermen on modern education', *School child*, 2 (1912), 7–8.

On Stephen Reynolds, *Seems so: a working-class view of politics* (London, 1911).

*251 'Education and the state, in relation to (a) curriculum, (b) finance, (c) division of control as between the central and local authority', *School government chronicle*, 87 (1912), 41–43.

252 'The educational significance of Hellerau', in *The eurhythmics of Jaques-Dalcroze*, edited by John W. Harvey (London: Constable, 1912), pp. 11–14.

Different from no. 327 below.

253   'Educational work in the mission field and at home', in *Christ and human need, being addresses delivered at a Conference on Foreign Missions and Social Problems, Liverpool, Jan. 2nd – 8th, 1912*, edited by Tissington Tatlow (London: Student Volunteer Missionary Union, 1912), pp. 119–29.

*254   'England's debt to German education', *Die neueren Sprachen: Zeitschrift für den neusprachlichen Unterricht*, 20 (1912), 321–25.

> Reprinted in Higginson, pp. 103–05. An abridged version is printed in *Bericht über die Verhandlungen der XV. Tagung des Allgemeinen Deutschen Neuphilologen-Verbandes (A.D.N.V.) in Frankfurt a. M. vom 27. bis 30. Mai 1912* (Heidelberg: Winter, 1913), and in *Welt-Warte: illustrierte internationale Zeitschrift für Kultur und Verkehr* [Wiesbaden], 15. Juni 1912.

*255   'England's debt to German education: Dr Sadler on von Humboldt' [letter], *Times educational supplement*, 1 Oct. 1912, pp. 111–12.

*256   'Examinations in secondary schools', *Educational times*, 1 Feb. 1912, pp. 69–70.

> Reprinted from *Indian education*, Sept. 1911 (see no. 105 above).

*257   'General report on the primary schools in Guernsey, 1911' [with J. W. Longsdon and others], in *Rapports sur les écoles publiques primaires, 1911* (Guernsey, 1912), pp. 4–23.

*258   'Hill, Thomas Wright', in *A cyclopedia of education*, edited by Paul Monroe, III (New York: Macmillan, 1912), pp. 278–80.

> Reprinted 1914. Sadler also contributed the following:

*259   'Hogg, Quintin', *ibid.*, pp. 300–01.

*260   'Huxley, Thomas Henry', *ibid.*, pp. 352–53.

*261   'Jowett, Benjamin', *ibid.*, pp. 570–71.

*262   'Kay-Shuttleworth, Sir James Phillips', *ibid.*, pp. 587-89.

*263   'The history of education', in *Germany in the nineteenth century: five lectures* [with J. H. Rose, C. H. Herford, and E. C. K. Gonner], University of Manchester publications, 65, Historical series, 13 (Manchester: University Press, 1912), pp. 101–27.

> Reprinted in Higginson, pp. 89–98. The whole book was re-issued in 1915 as *Germany in the nineteenth century: a series of lectures*, edited by C. H. Herford, University of Manchester publications, 96, Historical series, 25. A German translation appeared as *Deutschland im neunze-hnten Jahrhundert. fünf Vorlesungen . . .*, herausgegeben von C. H. Herford; ins Deutsche übertragen von Karl Breul (Berlin: Siegismund, 1913). Sadler's essay, 'Die Geschichte der Erziehung', occupies pp. 101–34.

264   'Spiritual influences in moral education', in *Mémoires sur l'éducation morale, présentés au deuxieme Congrès international d'éducation morale à La Haye, 22–27 août, 1912* (La Haye: Nijhoff, 1912), pp. 3–4.

> Translated as 'Godsdienst en zijn Invloed op de Zedelijke Opvoeding' in *Vlaamsch Opvoedkundig Tijdschrift*, 9 (1928), 453–54. This publication also contains translated extracts from *Our public elementary schools* (no. 430 below) and 'The educational outlook' (no. 446 below), as well as quotations from other works of Sadler's.

*265   'Thomas Godolphin Rooper', in *Dictionary of national biography, Second supplement* (1912), III, 228–29.

*266   'Von Humboldt and state influence' [letter], *Times educational supplement*, 6 August 1912, p. 87.

*267   'William Henry Herford', in *Dictionary of national biography, Second supplement* (1912), II, 255–56.

1913

*268   'All schools on a state list' [letter], *Journal of education*, n.s. 35 (1913), 771.

*269   'Deutscher Einfluss im englischen Erziehungswesen', *Magdeburgische Zeitung*, Kaisernummer, 15. Juni 1913.

*270 'Foreword', pp. 2–3, to [Catalogue of the] *International colour printing and poster exhibition, City Art Gallery, Leeds, February –April, 1913.*

*271 'Girls Public Day School Trust', *Athenaeum,* 15 Nov. 1913, p. 560.

*272 'Lithography in England' [letter], *Yorkshire post,* 14 Jan. 1913, p. 5.

*273 'Lord Haldane's hopes for English education', *Athenaeum,* 18 Jan. 1913, pp. 66–67.

*274 'Maurice, John Frederick Denison', in *A cyclopedia of education,* edited by Paul Monroe, IV (New York: Macmillan, 1913), pp. 160–61.

Sadler also contributed the following:

*275 'Newman, J. H.', *ibid.,* pp. 473–74.

276 'New hopes for education', *Daily news and leader,* 13 Jan. 1913, p. 6.

*277 'The pictures in the entrance-hall', *Gryphon,* 17 (1913–14), 18–19.

The University of Leeds magazine.

278 'Sunday schools and the state', *Sunday school chronicle,* 4 Dec. 1913, p. 1058.

*279 'Syndicalism and the teacher's work', *Times educational supplement,* 2 Dec. 1913, pp. 197–98.

*280 'Unresolved discords' [letter], [Parish magazine] of South Parade Baptist Church, Kirkstall Lane, Headingley, [Leeds], no. 47, Nov. 1913. pp. [2–5].

On discordant experiences in life. A slightly shorter version of no. 295 below.

1914

*281 'Before the War – and afterwards', *Times educational supplement*, 1 Dec. 1914, pp. 197–98.

An unsigned editorial.

*282 [Contribution to a discussion on the position of private schools in a national system of education], in *Report of the Conference of Educational Associations held at the University of London, January 1914* (1914), pp. 217–22.

Also printed in *Secondary education*, 2 Feb. 1914, pp. 41–43.

*283 'Education of a naval officer', *Manchester guardian*, 10 Oct. 1914, p. 6.

*284 'Educational ideals tested by the war', *School guardian*, 14 Nov. 1914, pp. 4–8.

*285 'English education in the seething-pot', *Athenaeum*, 17 Jan 1914, p. 105.

*286 ' "Leeds University: a criticism": electrical engineering departments in German and English universities' [letter], *Journal of education*, n.s. 36 (1914), 45.

In response to an article in the Dec. 1913 issue.

*287 *Modern Germany and the modern world* (London: Macmillan, 1914). 16 pp.

*288 'Note on Mr Greenwood's article on the Leeds municipal strike', *Economic journal*, 24 (1914), 146–52.

The article in question is printed immediately beforehand, on pp. 138–45. Sadler's article is reprinted in Higginson, pp. 101–03.

*289 'The outlook for 1914', *Times educational supplement*, 6 Jan. 1914, p. 11.

An unsigned editorial.

*290   'Post-impressionism and Prussian militarism' [letter], *Yorkshire post*, 21 Sept. 1914, p.6.

*291   'Preface', pp. ix–xiii, to *Boy life & labour: the manufacture of inefficiency*, by Arnold Freeman (London: King, 1914).

*292   *Reading in war time* (London: National Home-Reading Union, 1914). 12 pp.
       Also printed in *School government chronicle*, 92 (1914), 339–40.

*293   'Thoughts on present discontents in English education', *School government chronicle*, 91 (1914), 22–23.

*294   'Treitschke', *Manchester guardian*, 11 Nov. 1914, p. 12.
       A review of Adolf Hansrath, *Treitschke: his life and works* (London, 1914).

*295   'Unresolved discords', *Parents' review*, 25 (1914), 330–33.
       See no. 280 above.

1915

*296   'Arthur Francis Leach', *School world*, 17 (1915), 419–20.

297   'Back to the beginning', *Men's magazine* [Church of England Men's Society], no. 50 (Jan. 1915), pp. 19–23.

*298   'Changes in English education since 1900', in *Journal of proceedings and addresses of the fifty-third annual meeting and International Congress on Education held at Oakland, California, August 16–17, 1915* (Ann Arbor: National Education Association of the United States, 1915), pp. 144–48.
       Also printed in *School and society*, 11 Sept. 1915, pp. 367–71.

*299   'Education has saved the state', *Teacher's world*, 1 Sept. 1915, pp. 473–74.

300 'The educational task of England after the War', *School guardian*, 16 Oct. 1915, pp. 315–17.

301 'Examinations in secondary schools', *Secondary education*, Sept. 1915, pp. 91–92.

> Reprinted from *Indian education*, March 1915 (see no. 105 above).

*302 'The future of English education: morals of the war', *Times educational supplement*, 7 Dec. 1915, p. 142.

*303 'Government and the universities', *University magazine* [McGill University, Montreal], 14 (1915), 484–90.

> Reprinted in Higginson, pp. 105–07.

304 'If the Germans won: an article which every young man should read', *Evening news* [London], 10 Nov. 1915, p. 4.

*305 'The late Mr A. F. Leach: pioneer research worker', *The Times*, 1 Oct. 1915, p. 10.

*306 'Our public schools: after-war dangers', *Sunday times*, 19 Sept. 1915, p. 7.

*307 'The strength and weakness of German education', in *German culture: the contribution of the Germans to knowledge, literature, art, and life*, edited by W. P. Paterson (London: Jack, 1915), pp. 301–14.

*308 'Universities and the government', *T.P.'s weekly*, 4 Dec. 1915, pp. 557–58.

1916

*309 'The Chancellor', *Gryphon* [University of Leeds], 20 (1916–17), 18.

> On the Duke of Devonshire's appointment as Governor General of Canada.

*310 'The cross-currents in English education', *Edinburgh review*, 224 (1916), 340–60.

*311 'Education after the war' [letter], *Yorkshire observer*, 11 Sept. 1916, p.9.

*312 'The educational inquiry' [letter], *The Times*, 6 July 1916, p.8.

*313 'Educational links between Russia and Great Britain' [letter], *Manchester guardian*, 5 July 1916, p. 7.

*314 'An English education for England', *Contemporary review*, 110 (1916), 273–89.
> Reprinted in Higginson, pp. 110–16.

*315 'The government and education', *School guardian*, 16 Sept. 1916, pp. 245–47.

*316 'The government and education', *Today*, 16 Dec. 1916, pp. 155–56.

*317 'Letter from the Vice-Chancellors of the Universities of Manchester, Liverpool, Leeds and Sheffield to the Joint Secretaries of the Committee on Public Retrenchment' [with F. E. Weiss, Alfred Dale, and H. A. L. Fisher], in *The University of Leeds: twelfth report, 1915–16* (Leeds, 1916), pp. 75–82.
> The letter is dated August 1915.

*318 'Lord Haldane on education' [letter], *The Times*, 14 July 1916, p. 7.

*319 'Need we imitate German education?' *The Times on war and education*, 14 Jan. 1916, p. 3.
> Issued with *The Times* of the same date.

320 'Our greatest need — educational reform', *Teacher's world*, 19 July 1916, pp. 425–26.

321 'Preface', pp. 5–6, to *Jugoslav nationalism: three lectures*, by Bogumil Vosnjak (London: Polsue, [1916]).

"An address delivered by M. E. Sadler on Kossovo Day, 1916".

*322 'Should education have a separate organ of local government? Notes on English experience since 1902', *Scottish class teacher*, 17 (1916), 69–71.

*323 'Training the nation to meet the hard days to come', *Yorkshire evening post*, 27 July 1916, p. 6.

324 'The universities and the war', in *The Empire and the future: a series of imperial studies lectures delivered in the University of London, King's College* (London: Macmillan, 1916), pp. 1–9.

*325 'Visitors from France', *Gryphon* [University of Leeds], 19 (1915–16), 82–83.

On the visit to the University of a delegation from French universities.

1917

*326 'An artist's rooms', *Manchester guardian*, 8 Oct. 1917, p. 8.

On the painter Matthew Maris. Reprinted in Sadleir, pp. 306–08.

327 'Introduction', pp. 9–11, to *The eurhythmics of Jaques-Dalcroze*, edited by John W. Harvey, second and revised edition (London: Constable, 1917).

Different from no. 252 above.

*328 'Magic of Matthew Maris: a hermit from the world', *The Times*, 25 August 1917, p. 9.

† 'Parallel movements in German and English education since the beginning of the war'.

See no. 105 above.

*329   'Science, pure and applied' [letter], *Manchester guardian*, 22 August 1917, p. 3.

*330   'Science, pure and applied' [letter], *Manchester guardian*, 4 Sept. 1917, p. 8.

   In answer to a criticism of the previous letter (no. 329 above) by J. W. McConnel.

*331   'The state and education' [letter], *New statesman*, 22 Sept. 1917, pp. 588–89.

*332   *Technical education and scientific research, with special reference to the needs of the leather industries: an address delivered ... to the members of the United Tanners' Federation at the Leather-sellers' Hall, July 17th, 1917.* 12 pp.

*333   'Universities and industrial research' [letter], *New statesman*, 6 Oct. 1917, p. 12.

   Reprinted in *Journal of the British Science Guild*, 6 (1917), 16–17.

1918

*334   'Benares and Sarnath', *Gryphon* [University of Leeds], 21 (1917–18), 54.

   The Indian cities.

*335   'Introduction', pp. 7–16, to *The German school as a war nursery,* ... by V. H. Friedel (London: Melrose, 1918).

 336   'Modern languages and modern business', *Bankers magazine* [New York], 97 (1918), 594–98.

1919

*337   *The educational movement in India and Britain: an address delivered ... to the Senate of the University of Bombay ... April 4, 1919* (Bombay, 1919). 15 pp.

Reprinted in *Sir Michael Sadler: a centenary brochure, July 3, 1961,*
[compiled by J. H. Higginson] (Leeds, 1961), and in Higginson
pp. 132–36.

338   'The educational outlook in England', *Collegian* [Calcutta], 12
      (1919), 5–6.

*339 'A new chapter in our history: the Vice-Chancellor's message',
      Gryphon [University of Leeds], n.s. 1 (1919–20), 3.

*340 *Report,* [of the] Calcutta University Commission, 1917–19, 13 vols
      (Calcutta: Superintendent Government Printing, India, 1919).

      Sadler was President of the Commission. Vols 1–5, the Report; vol. 6,
      Appendices; vols 7–13, Evidence and documents. Vols 1–5 were also
      issued as *Report of the Commission appointed by the Government of
      India to enquire into the condition and prospects of the University of
      Calcutta,* Cmd. 386–90 (London: H.M.S.O., 1919). The Superintendent
      Government Printing, India, also issued *Selected chapters of the report
      of the Calcutta University Commission* (Calcutta, 1919).

1920

*341 'Education for the new era', *Gryphon* [University of Leeds], n.s. 1
      (1919–20), 51.
      On an address at Leeds University, 16 Feb. 1920, by F. W. Sanderson.

*342 'The intellectual ferment in India', *East and the West,* 18 (1920),
      289–93.

*343 'Professor Strong on recent developments in Scottish education',
      Gryphon [University of Leeds], n.s. 1 (1919–20), 51.

344   'Village education in India', *International review of missions,* 9
      (1920), 495–516.

1921

*345 'Agricultural education in Yorkshire' [letter], *Yorkshire post,* 16
      Dec. 1921, p. 5.

*346　'The classics in education: a notable report', *Yorkshire observer*, 20 July 1921, p. 8.

> Signed "By a special contributor". On the *Report of the Committee appointed by the Prime Minister to inquire into the position of the classics in the educational system of the United Kingdom* (H.M.S.O., 1921).

*347　'The dual system' [letter], *Times educational supplement*, 17 Dec. 1921, p. 567.

> On the place of denominational schools in the educational system.

*348　'An early suggestion for a university in Leeds', *Gryphon* [University of Leeds], n.s. 2 (1920–21), 117–18.

　349　'Education for life and duty', *International review of missions*, 10 (1921), 449–66.

*350　'The financial position of the University', *Gryphon* [University of Leeds], n.s. 2 (1920–21), 109–10.

*351　'The future of Leeds University: pure and applied science departments', *Leeds mercury*, 14 July 1921, p. 10.

*352　'Future of Leeds University: will it survive modern industrialism?', *Leeds mercury*, 13 July 1921, p. 7.

*353　'Haphazard retrenchment in education' [letter], *Yorkshire evening post*, 23 Dec. 1921, p. 3.

　354　*In memoriam Harry Behrens, born February 18th 1854, died October 20th 1921: an address given ... at the memorial service in the Cartwright Hall, Bradford, October 25th, 1921.* 4 pp.

*355　'The late Miss C. Clarkson', *Yorkshire post*, 2 June 1921, p. 6.

*356　'The late Mr R. Brazier', *The Times*, 18 July 1921, p. 13.

*357　'Leeds Town Hall' [letter], *Westminster gazette*, 28 Nov. 1921, p.2.

> On the mural decorations.

*358 'Leeds Town Hall decorations' [letter], *Yorkshire post*, 26 Nov. 1921, p. 12.

*359 'New universities: will they survive?', *Pall Mall and globe*, 21 July 1921, p. 6.

*360 'The new young', *St Martin-in-the-Fields review*, no. 366 (August 1921), pp. 371–72.
> Reprinted in Higginson, pp. 137–38.

*361 'A poet of trees and woodland: Mr John Freeman's visit', *Yorkshire observer*, 25 Oct. 1921, p. 6.
> Unsigned.

*362 'The poetry of John Freeman: his visit to Leeds', *Yorkshire post*, 29 Oct. 1921, p. 8.

*363 'The revolt of the young: why boys and girls demand more freedom and responsibility', *Evening standard* [London], 3 August 1921, p. 5.
> Also printed in the *Manchester evening chronicle* of the same date, under the headline 'No coddling day for youth: why they demand more freedom'.

*364 'Science and agriculture' [letter], *New statesman*, 12 Nov. 1921, p.165.

*365 'The silhouette of Leeds: an architectural treasure ground', *Yorkshire post*, 4 August 1921, p.4.
> Signed "Contributed by one of a small party that spent Bank Holiday in inspecting some of the Leeds churches and public buildings".

*366 'Sir C. J. Holmes and Yorkshire', *Yorkshire post*, 21 Nov. 1921, p. 5.

*367 'The teaching of history', *Westminster gazette*, 16 July 1921, p. 8.

*368   'The universities and adult education: extra-mural work', in *Second Congress of the Universities of the Empire, 1921: report of proceedings*, edited by Alex Hill (London: Bell, for the Universities Bureau of the British Empire, 1921), pp. 160–63.

The volume also contains:

*369   [Contribution to a discussion on university finance], *ibid.*, pp. 329–32.

*370   'The University motto' [letter], *Gryphon* [University of Leeds], n.s. 3 (1921–22), 13.

*371   'The University of Leeds and women' [letter], *Yorkshire observer*, 15 Dec. 1921, p. 11.

*372   'The University of Leeds: place of Greek in modern study', *Leeds mercury*, 20 July 1921, p. 6.

*373   'We need security and freedom', *Daily Malta chronicle*, 1 Nov. 1921, p. 11.

On the occasion of Malta's new constitution.

*374   'The Yorkshire of our dreams', *Yorkshire weekly post*, 10 Dec. 1921, p. 21.

1922

*375   'Adult education', *School government chronicle*, 108 (1922), 88–89.

*376   'The art of the East and the mind of the West', *Yorkshire post*, 30 Oct. 1922, p. 7.

*377   'Brains in nursing', *Nursing times*, 21 Jan. 1922, p. 54.

*378   'A Christmas Eve centenary: Matthew Arnold, poet and critic: his service to education', *Yorkshire post*, 22 Dec. 1922, p. 6.

Also printed in the *Nottingham guardian*, 23 Dec. 1922, p. 4.

*379   [Contributions to discussion on the increase of residential accommodation for undergraduate and other students], in *Abridged report of proceedings [of the] annual Conference of the Universities of Great Britain & Ireland, 1922* (London: Universities Bureau of the British Empire, [n.d.]), pp. 13–14, 17–18.

*380   'Discriminating repairs', *Yorkshire post*, 8 Dec. 1922, p. 5.
        On the need for change in various English institutions, including the educational system.

*381   'The English and their schools: the price of timidity: a braver spirit for the new age', *Observer*, 22 Jan. 1922, p. 7.

*382   'The late Miss Cleghorn', *Sheffield daily telegraph*, 8 Dec. 1922, p. 6.

*383   'A reduced grant to the universities' [letter], *Spectator*, 14 Jan. 1922, p. 46.

*384   'Sanderson of Oundle: a creative mind in English education', *Nineteenth century and after*, 92 (1922), 943–52.

*385   'Suggested commission on education' [letter], *The Times,* 25 Oct. 1922, p. 13.

*386   'A threefold allegiance', *University bulletin*, 1 (1922), 2.
        On the role of the Association of University Teachers.

1923

*387   ' "Character makes character" ', *Scouter*, 17 (1923), 204, 206.

*388   'Charlotte Mason', *Parents' review*, 34 (1923), 217–19.

*389   'Introduction', pp. 11–14, to *Catalogue of an exhibition of works by Vincent Van Gogh (1853–1890), [at] Ernest Brown & Phillips, The Leicester Galleries, Leicester Square, 1923.*

*390 'Introduction', pp. vii–x, to *The life and work of Sir James Kay-Shuttleworth*, by Frank Smith (London: Murray, 1923).

*391 'Matthew Arnold', *Nineteenth century and after*, 93 (1923), 199–207, 366–77.

> In two parts.

*392 'Matthew Arnold and the modern universities', *Gryphon* [University of Leeds], n.s. 4 (1922–23), 206–07.

*393 'The memorial sculpture at Leeds: Sir Michael Sadler's view', *Yorkshire post*, 26 May 1923, p. 8.

> A statement to the press about Eric Gill's sculpture at Leeds University. Also printed in the *Leeds mercury* of the same date.

*394 'Mr Frederick Dawson on William Baines', *Gryphon* [University of Leeds], n.s. 4 (1922–23), 163.

*395 'A nineteenth century experiment in education: the work of Matthew and Rowland Hill', *Forum of education*, 1 (1923), 14–26.

396 [Presidential address], in *Report of the eleventh annual Conference of Educational Associations held at the University College, London, December 1922 and January 1923* (London: Conference Committee, 1923), pp. 1–18.

> On Mrs Sherwood's *The Fairchild family.*
> The *Report* also contains:

397 'The growth of bureaucracy in education', *ibid.*, pp. 129–30.

> The opening paper of a discussion (subheading: 'Précis').

398 'An educational experiment in Birmingham: the work of the Hills for English education', *ibid.*, pp. 287–90.

> On Rowland and Matthew Davenport Hill (subheading: 'An abstract').

*399 'The science of childhood', *World's children*, 3 (1923), 134–37.

*400 'Sir Michael Sadler and private schools' [letter], *Bradford daily telegraph*, 8 Jan. 1923, p. 5.

*401   'William Gilpin' [letter], *Nation & the Athenaeum*, 20 Jan. 1923, p. 611.

1924

402   'Education and letters', in *The life-work of Lord Avebury (Sir John Lubbock), 1834–1913*, ... edited by his daughter, the Hon. Mrs Adrian Grant Duff (London: Watts, 1924), pp. 196–224.

*403   'Education and life', in *Education and life: addresses delivered at the National Conference on Education and Citizenship held at Toronto, Canada, April, 1923*, edited by J. A. Dale (Toronto: Oxford University Press, 1924), pp. 245–55.

> Sadler also contributed:

*404   'A liberal education and its cost', *ibid.*, pp. 270–78.

*405   'Personality and character', *ibid.*, pp. 192–200.

*406   'Tradition and freedom', *ibid.*, pp. 17–28.

*407   'The English in Canada', *Weekly Westminster*, 19 Jan. 1924, p. 370.

*408   'Introduction', pp. vii–viii, to *Christian education in Africa and the East*, [by J. H. Oldham and others] (London: Student Christian Movement, 1924).

*409   'Mr Lewis Paton and Manchester', *Oxford magazine*, 28 Feb. 1924, p. 321.

*410   'The Principal of St. Hugh's, *Oxford magazine*, 8 May 1924, pp. 420–21.

> Miss E. F. Jourdain. Unsigned.

411   'Progress of education in England, 1823–1923', in *Birkbeck College centenary lectures: a course of lectures given at the College in connection with the celebration of the centenary* (London: University of London Press, 1924), pp. 65–83.

*412   'Religion and national life', in *Education and religion: a course of lectures given in Bristol Cathedral*, edited ... by E. A. Burroughs (London: Hodder and Stoughton, [1924]), pp. 73–89.

       Preface dated 1924.

*413   'University of Leeds: science and arts in Yorkshire: jubilee celebrations', *The Times*, 15 Dec. 1924, pp. 15–16.

*414   *What is a liberal education? Report of an address ... at Leighton Park School on 6th June, 1924.* 10 pp.

1925

*415   'Art in education', *Architectural review*, 57 (1925), 93–94.

416   'Roland Strasser and his art', *Apollo*, 1 (1925), 9–12.

*417   'The wall-paintings of Ajanta', *Weekly Westminster*, 27 June 1925, p. 228.

       A review of Sri Mukul Chandra Dey, *My pilgrimages to Ajanta and Pagh* (London, 1925).

*418   'What the future holds: no. 15, Education', *Graphic*, 6 June 1925, p. 950.

1926

*419   'The coal crisis' [letter, with others], *The Times*, 3 May 1926, p. 15.

420 'Education and the things of the spirit', in *Bootham School, 1823–1923* [edited by F. E. Pollard] (London: Dent, 1926), pp. vii–xiii.

421 'Foreword', pp. 7–10, to *Richard Green Moulton: professor of literary theory and interpretation in the University of Chicago: a memoir*, by William Fiddian Moulton (London: Epworth Press, 1926).

422 *The future of the Bodleian* (Oxford University Press, 1926) 12 pp.
    No author statement. Attributed to Sadler in Sadleir, p. 351.

*423 'Greetings', *Army schoolmistress*, Dec. 1926, p. 4.
    On Pestalozzi.

*424 'Harold Spender', *Oxford magazine*, 29 April 1926, p. 404.

*425 'In the days of my youth', *T.P.'s and Cassell's weekly*, 3 July 1926, pp. 342, 350.
    Reprinted in Higginson, p. 11.

*426 'Introduction', p. iii, to *Bilingualism (with special reference to Bengal)*, by Michael West, Bureau of Education, India, Occasional reports, 13 (Calcutta: Government of India, 1926).

*427 'Introduction', pp. xi–xvi, to *Four essentials of education*, by Thomas Jesse Jones (New York: Scribner, 1926).
    Reprinted in Higginson, pp. 143–45.

*428 'Introduction', pp. 5–8, to *The folk high schools of Denmark and the development of a farming community*, by Holger Begtrup, Hans Lund, Peter Manniche (London: Oxford University Press, 1926).
    New edition, 1929; 3rd edition, 1936; 4th edition, 1949.

*429 'Miss Mary Beard', *Manchester guardian*, 9 Nov. 1926, p. 18.

*430 *Our public elementary schools* (London: Thornton Butterworth, 1926). 90 pp.

431 'Preface', pp. 12–13, to *The Handbook of the Education Week held in the City of Bradford, March 21st–27th, 1926* (Bradford Education Committee, [n.d.]).

*432 'Sir Arthur Acland', *Oxford magazine*, 21 Oct. 1926, pp. 13–14.
Reprinted in Higginson, pp. 13–14.

*433 'Sturry Court' [letter], *The Times*, 9 June 1926, p. 12.

1927

*434 'The beauties of Oxford' [letter], *The Times*, 29 Oct. 1927, p. 13.

*435 'The Indian inquiry' [letter], *The Times*, 29 Nov. 1927, p. 12.

*436 'The Indian inquiry: suggestions for the Commissioners' [letter], *The Times*, 10 Nov. 1927, p. 15.

*437 'Municipalities and art' [letter], *Yorkshire post,* 30 Nov. 1927, p. 3.

*438 'Pestalozzi, 1746–1827', *Parents' review*, 38 (1927), 116–18.

*439 'Thomas William Jex-Blake', in *Dictionary of national biography, 1912–1921* (1927), pp. 298–99.

1928

*440 'The alleged dullness of writers on education', *Nineteenth century and after*, 103 (1928), 365–74.

441 'The Bodleian', *Oxford magazine*, 46 (1928), 436.

*442 'The Bodleian' [letter], *The Times*, 8 Feb. 1928, p. 10.

*443 'The Bodleian' [letter], *The Times*, 13 Feb. 1928, p. 8.

*444 'Bodley's Library' [letter, with others], *The Times*, 18 Feb. 1928, p. 13.

*445 'The different idioms in modern painting', *Barbizon House record*, 10 (1928), 21–24.

*446 'The educational outlook: presidential address', in *Report of the sixteenth annual Conference of Educational Associations held at the University College, London, January 1928* (Conference Committee, 1928), pp. 2–16.
    Reprinted in Higginson, pp. 150–56.
    The *Report* also contains:

*447 'The alleged dullness of writers on education', *ibid.*, pp. 210–11.

*448 'Linking-up in adolescent education', *ibid.*, pp. 49–51.
    Introducing a discussion.

*449 'Oral tests and the speaking of English', *ibid.*, pp. 17–18.
    An informal report of the opening paper of a discussion.

*450 'The examination system' [letter], *The Times*, 20 Oct. 1928, p. 8.

*451 'Introduction', pp. ix–lii, to *Dr Arnold of Rugby*, by Arnold Whitridge (London: Constable, 1928).

*452 'The jeopardy of Oxford', *London mercury*, 17 (1928), 545–55.

*453 [Professor H. R. Procter], *Journal of the International Society of Leather Trades' Chemists*, 12 (1928), 106.

*454 *Shaftesbury: reformer and reconciler: the seventh Shaftesbury lecture delivered on Monday, 7th May, 1928 ... in Kingsgate Chapel, London* (London: Shaftesbury Society & Ragged School Union, [n.d.]). 13 pp.

*455 *Thomas Day: an English disciple of Rousseau*, The Rede lecture, 1928 (Cambridge: University Press, 1928). 47 pp.

1929

*456 'Biologists for the Empire' [letter], *The Times*, 14 Jan. 1929, p. 8.

457 'Cambridge and Oxford' [letter], *Education*, 6 Dec. 1929, p. 528.

*458 'Changing Oxford: future of Radcliffe Observatory' [letter], *The Times*, 26 Nov. 1929, p. 12.

*459 'The educational needs of England', *English review*, 48 (1929), 27–37.

460 'Examination dangers at Oxford', *Oxford mail*, 23 Nov. 1929, p. 5.

*461 'Examinations', *New era*, 10 (1929), 9–19.

462 'Examinations', *Nation and Athenaeum*, 19 Jan. 1929, pp. 550–51.

*463 'Examinations' [letter], *Nation and Athenaeum*, 2 Feb. 1929, p. 612.

*464 'Films in education: travel and nature study: value of visual instruction', *The Times film number*, 19 March 1929, p. vii.

Issued with *The Times* of the same date.

*465 'Foreword', pp. ix–x, to *Everyday art at school & home: a book for children, parents, teachers and students,* by D. D. Sawer (London: Batsford, 1929).

*466 'The liberal education' [letter], *New statesman*, 28 Dec. 1929, p. 390.

467 *The new English countryside: its development and beauty.* 4 pp.

Setting out the aims of a conference with this title to be held at University College, Oxford, on 18 January 1930. Dated December 18, 1929.

*468   'New schemes for schools: what is a liberal education?' [letter], *The Times*, 17 Dec. 1929, p. 10.

469   'Oxford and Cambridge' [letter], *Sunday times*, 8 Dec. 1929, p. 12.

470   'Oxford and Cambridge compared' [letter], *Country life*, 28 Dec. 1929, p. 940.

*471   'Pageant of Italian painting: the prestige of great pictures and one which should be bought for the nation', *Oxford mail*, 31 Dec. 1929, p. 4.

   Also printed in *Yorkshire observer*, 31 Dec. 1929, p. 6, as 'Great pageant of Italian painting'.

*472   'The profession of commerce: approach from the universities: questions to Oxford tutors' [letter], *The Times*, 28 Dec. 1929, p. 9.

*473   'St Aldate's, Oxford' [letter, with H. A. L. Fisher], *The Times*, 3 August 1929, p. 6.

*474   'The story of education in Manchester', in *The soul of Manchester*, edited by W. H. Brindley (Manchester: University Press, 1929), pp. 39–61.

*475   'Success in trade: contact with markets: a question of English psychology' [letter], *The Times*, 10 Dec. 1929, p. 17.

*476   'Ten years later', *Calcutta review*, 30 (1929), 1–7.

   On the work of the Calcutta University Commission (see no. 340 above).

*477   'A unique exhibition: Dutch art in London', *Oxford evening times*, 4 Jan. 1929, p. 2.

478   'When did England first get "education"?' [letter], *Oxford evening times*, 15 Jan. 1929, p. 5.

1930

*479 'Agriculture and medicine' [letter, with others], *The Times*, 5 Feb. 1930, p. 10.

480 'Beheading country schools', *Countryman*, April 1930, pp. 25–28.

481 *The City of Oxford School* [with A. D. Lindsay and C. Cookson]. 7 pp.

> Dated May 1930.

*482 'Edward Baines', in *Encyclopaedia of the social sciences*, II (1930), p. 391.

> On both Edward Baines the elder (1774–1848) and the younger (1800–90).

483 'The English state and the schools' [letter], *Nation and Athenaeum*, 22 Feb. 1930, pp. 697–98.

*484 'An Englishman's thoughts on the service of American education to the world', *Schoolmen's week* [University of Pennsylvania], 3 April 1930, pp. 4–12.

485 'The future of the countryside', *Observer*, 19 Jan. 1930, p. 15.

*486 'Introduction', pp. 9–14, to *The Mongolian horde*, by Roland Strasser; translated from the German by 'R.T.G.' (London: Cape, 1930).

*487 'Introduction', pp. xi–xvii, to *Towards a new education: a record and synthesis of the discussions on the new psychology and the curriculum at the fifth world conference of the New Education Fellowship, held at Elsinore, Denmark, in August 1929*, edited ... by William Boyd ... (London: Knopf, 1930).

† 'Liberal education'

> See no. 491 below.

*488   'Miss Emily Ford', *The Times*, 7 March 1930, p. 21.

*489   'Miss Lucy Martineau', *The Times*, 22 Jan. 1930, p. 19.

*490   'Mr A. G. Lupton', *The Times,* 11 Feb. 1930, p. 16.

*491   *The outlook in secondary education*, Julius and Rosa Sachs
        Endowment Fund lectures, 2 (New York: Teachers College,
        Columbia University, 1930). iii, 56 pp.

> Three lectures, printed separately in *Teachers College record*, 32
> (1930–31), 1–16, 123–39, and 256–78, as 'Progress and pitfalls', 'Youth
> and tests', and 'Liberal education'. The first was also published in
> *School and society*, 5 April 1930, pp. 443–52.

*492   'The philosophy underlying the system of education in England,
        part 1', in *Educational yearbook of the International Institute
        of Teachers College, Columbia University, 1929*, edited by
        I. L. Kandel (New York: Teachers College, 1930), pp. 3–74.

493   'Poetry for success in business', *Everyman*, 30 Jan. 1930, p. 5.

494   'The primitive in some English people', *Oversea education,* 1
        (1930), 73–78.

*495   'Professor Joseph Wright', *The Times*, 4 March 1930, p. 11.

  †   'Progress and pitfalls'
        See no. 491 above.

496   *St Mary the Virgin, Oxford: the University Church* [with Herbert
        E. D. Blakiston]. 2 pp.

> A letter addressed to the Restoration Committee and the Parochial
> Church Council. 1930 is the date suggested by the British Museum
> *General catalogue of printed books.*

497   'Success in business', *Everyman*, 16 Jan. 1930, p. 699.

498   'What are the universities for?', *Saturday review*, 1 March 1930,
        pp. 261–62.

  †   'Youth and tests'
        See no. 491 above.

1931

*499   'British universities today: (11) Leeds', *Discovery*, 12 (1931), 78–83.

*500   [Contribution to discussion on conditions of admission to universities and their effects], in *Fourth Congress of the Universities of the Empire, 1931: report of proceedings* (London: Bell, for the Universities Bureau of the British Empire, 1931), pp. 129–33.

*501   [Contribution to] 'The things that Britain does best', *Today and tomorrow*, 2 (1931), 11–12.

*502   'Education for the African child', *World's children*, 11 (1931), 165.

*503   'Education in a changing world', in *Education in a changing commonwealth: report of a British Commonwealth education conference held in London in July 1931*, edited by Wyatt Rawson (London: New Education Fellowship, 1931), pp. 3–5.

Also printed, as 'Education in a changing Commonwealth', in *New era in home and school*, 12 (1931), 300–01.

*504   'The English philosophy of education', *Internationale Zeitschrift für Erziehungswissenschaft / International education review*, 1 (1931–32), 350–59.

Reprinted in Higginson, pp. 156–58.

*505   'The examination system', *New ideals quarterly*, 5 (1931), 43–48.

506   'Examinations in English education', in *Conference on examinations, under the auspices of the Carnegie Corporation, the Carnegie Foundation, and the International Institute of Teachers College, Columbia University ... Grand Hotel, Eastbourne, England, May 23, 24, 25, 1931, ...* edited by Paul Monroe (New York: Teachers College, 1931), pp. 267–70.

507   'Introduction', pp. vii–xii, to *Ruskin's Guild of St George*, by Edith Hope Scott (London: Methuen, 1931).

508 'Mr Epstein's Genesis', [letter], *New statesman*, 21 Feb. 1931, p. 584.

*509 'Mr Owen Merton', *The Times*, 30 Jan. 1931, p. 19.

*510 'Mrs John Dymond', *The Times*, 2 April 1931, p. 15.

*511 *The only tragedy: an exchange of letters between Sir Michael E. Sadler, Master of University College, Oxford, and Elmer Ellsworth Brown, Chancellor of New York University* ... (New York: New York University, 1931). 27 pp.

*512 'Pablo Picasso', *Artwork*, 7 (1931), 153–54.

*513 'R. B. Davis sporting landscapes' [letter], *Sunday times*, 20 Dec. 1931, p. 8.

*514 'Richard Lovell Edgeworth', in *Encyclopaedia of the social sciences*, V (1931), pp. 398–99.
      Deals also with Maria Edgeworth.

*515 'Saving Oxford's fair face', *Listener*, 24 June 1931, pp. 1053–56.

*516 'Spelling reform — further comments', *Listener*, 2 Sept. 1931, p. 375.

1932

*517 [Address at the annual meeting of the Dalcroze Society], in *Report of the twentieth annual Conference of Educational Associations held at the University College, London, January 1932* (Conference Committee, 1932), pp. 104–09.
      Also printed in *Journal of the Dalcroze Society*, no. 16 (May 1932), pp. 9–11.

*518 'Benjamin Jowett', in *Encyclopaedia of the social sciences*, VIII (1932), pp. 428–29.

*519   'Body, mind and bridle: an integrated education', *Modern church-man*, 21 (1931–32), 589–95.

*520   [Contribution to a discussion on the establishment of a central institute for imperial education], in *Report of the centenary meeting [of the] British Association for the Advancement of Science, London, September 23–30 1931* (London: the Association, 1932), pp. 502–03.

*521   'Creative economy in education', *Observer*, 16 Oct. 1932, p. 8.
       A review of L. P. Jacks, *Education through recreation* (London, 1932).

*522   'Crisis in universities', *Observer*, 13 Nov. 1932, p. 9.
       A review of Walter M. Kotschnig and Elined Prys, ed., *The university in a changing world: a symposium* (London, 1932).

*523   'Dr Georg Kerschensteiner', *The Times*, 26 Jan. 1932, p. 14.
       Reprinted in Higginson, p. 81.

*524   'Dr Robert Eisler's lecture on currency', *Oxford magazine*, 28 Jan. 1932, pp. 348–49.

*525   *Is a change coming in education? The Frank Metcalfe memorial lecture, 1932, delivered in the Speech Room at Rugby School, September 23rd, 1932* (London: National Adult School Union, [n.d.]). 26 pp.

*526   'Leeds', *Heaton review*, 5 (1932), 7–10.

*527   'Liberal education and modern business', *Journal of the Textile Institute*, 23 (1932), 85–93.

*528   *A liberal education for all: an address given March 27, 1932, in Exeter College, Oxford, at the Easter Study School of the League of Industry* (London: League of Industry, 1932). 16 pp.

*529   *Liberal education for everybody: the Essex Hall lecture, 1932* (London: the Lindsey Press, [n.d.]). 50 pp.

*530   *Modern art and revolution*, Day to day pamphlets, 13 (London: Woolf, 1932). 32 pp.

*531   'Modern languages in schools' [letter], *The Times*, 29 Sept. 1932, p. 6.

*532   'Mr John Bickersteth', *The Times*, 27 Sept. 1932, p. 9.

*533   [Obituary tribute to C. P. Scott], *Manchester guardian*, 9 Jan. 1932, p. 13.

*534   'Professor Graham Wallas', *The Times*, 13 August 1932, p. 10.

535   'Schools in the English countryside', *Spectator*, 9 April 1932, pp. 499–501.

*536   'Secondary school fees: contributions from parents: terms of new circular' [letter], *The Times*, 26 Oct. 1932, p. 13.

*537   'Sir James Kay-Shuttleworth', in *Encyclopaedia of the social sciences*, VIII (1932), pp. 552–53.

*538   'Teaching as a branch of the Civil Service', *Journal of education*, 64 (1932), 79–81.

1933

539   'Education in China', *Oversea education*, 4 (1933), 53–62.

*540   'For students of all nations: a club in London' [letter, with others], *The Times*, 26 Jan. 1933, p. 8.

*541   'Foreword', pp. 5–6, to *Heaton review*, 6 (1933).
       The *Heaton review* was "a northern miscellany of art and literature".

542 'A full time in free time: the organisation of leisure', *Playing fields journal*, 2 (1932–33), 75–83.

> A review article on L. P. Jacks, *Education through recreation* (London, 1932).

*543 'Heavy traffic in Oxford: damage to college buildings: vertical vibrations measured' [letter, with H. A. L. Fisher], *The Times*, 9 Dec. 1933, p. 13.

*544 'The need for a biological outlook', *Discovery*, 14 (1933), 11–12.

*545 'Osteopathy' [letter], *The Times*, 3 Nov. 1933, p. 15.

*546 'The outlook', *Oxford magazine*, 26 Oct. 1933, pp. 95–97.

> The international outlook. Reprinted in Higginson, pp. 163-65.

*547 'Preface', pp. ix–x, to *Retrospect and prospect: sixty years of women's education,* by Sara A. Burstall (London: Longmans, 1933).

*548 'This age of broadcasting', *Radio times*, 22 Dec. 1933, p. 877.

1934

549 'Address', *Town and country planning*, 2 (1933–34), 140–42.

> On the Oxford Preservation Trust.

*550 'Dr Farnell's memories', *Observer*, 3 June 1934, p. 8.

> A review of Lewis R. Farnell, *An Oxonian looks back* (London, 1934).

*551 'Education of choristers' [letter], *The Times*, 18 Oct. 1934, p. 8.

*552 'Elite by examination?', *Schoolmaster & woman teacher's chronicle*, 8 Nov. 1934, p. 658.

> See also no. 553 below.

*553   'English snobbery and the future: misgivings after reading Mr Spikes', *Schoolmaster & woman teacher's chronicle,* 22 Nov. 1934, p. 737.

> On a published response to 'Elite by examination?' (no. 552 above) by W. H. Spikes.

*554   'Foreword', p. v, to *The birth of a university: a passage in the life of E. A. Sonnenschein,* by E. J. Somerset (Oxford: Blackwell, 1934).

> The University of Birmingham.

*555   'Foreword', pp. v–vi [with Sir Philip Hartog], to *An English bibliography of examinations (1900–1932),* by Mary C. Champneys, International Institute Examinations Enquiry (London: Macmillan, 1934).

> Sadler also contributed:

*556   'Publications bearing on the general history of education with special reference to examinations', *ibid.,* pp. xviii–xxiv.

557   'The future of the universities', *Daily telegraph,* 30 Oct. 1934, p. 14.

*558   'Introduction', p. [iii], to *Tagore at Shantinekatan, or A survey of Dr Rabindranath Tagore's educational experiments at Shantinekatan (Bengal, India),* by H. Chaturvedi (Bombay: Mathai, [1934]).

> Introduction dated 1934.

*559   'Mr A. J. Pressland', *The Times,* 11 Oct. 1934, p. 19.

*560   'Oxford in danger', *Oxford,* 1 no. 2 (Winter 1934), 50–59.

*561   'Oxford: preservation and progress: a practical plan: the solution of the traffic problem', *Manchester guardian,* 29 Oct. 1934, pp. 9–10.

*562   'Preservation of Oxford' [letter, with H. A. L. Fisher], *The Times,* 3 Nov. 1934, p. 13.

*563 'Roger Fry: an appreciation', *Life and letters*, 11 (1934), 14–20.

*564 'Ruskin and Oxford' [letter], *The Times*, 10 Oct. 1934, p. 10.

*565 'The scholar gipsy', *Oxford magazine*, 25 Jan. 1934, pp. 366–67.

   Unsigned. On the form of the story found in Joseph Glanvill's *Vanity of Dogmatising.*

566 'This England', *Time and tide*, 24 Nov. 1934, p. 1512.

   A review of Odette Keun, *I discover the English* (London, 1934).

567 'The two-mindedness of England' [letter], *Time and tide,* 6 Oct. 1934, p. 1223.

1935

568 *Arts of West Africa (excluding music)* [editor] (London: Oxford University Press, for the International Institute of African Languages and Cultures, 1935). xi, 101 pp.; plates.

   Sadler contributed the following:

569 'Bibliography relating to indigenous art in tropical Africa', *ibid.,* pp. 97–101.

570 'Significance and vitality of African art', *ibid.,* pp. 1–12.

*571 'An educational exhibition' [letter], *The Times*, 15 August 1935, p. 11.

*572 'The Group movement: a valuation — I', *Spectator*, 11 Oct. 1935, pp. 541–42.

*573 'Intellectual and political backgrounds: twenty-five years' retrospect', *Times educational supplement*, 7 Sept. 1935, p. 315.

   Reprinted in Higginson, pp. 179–81.

*574   *John Adams: a lecture in his memory: being the second John Adams lecture given in the Institute,* University of London, Institute of Education, Studies and reports, 6 (London: Oxford University Press, for the Institute of Education, 1935). 18 pp.

Reprinted in Higginson, pp. 172–75.

575   'The scope and purpose of education', *Friend,* 6 Sept. 1935, pp. 799–802.

576   *The spiritual elements in education: the Winifred Mercier memorial lecture at Whitelands College, Putney, November 10th, 1935.* 24 pp.

*577   'Universities and corporate life', in *Synchronised conferences of the World Federation of Educational Associations, the International Federation of Associations of Secondary Teachers, and the International Federation of Teachers' Associations, Oxford, 10th–17th August 1935: report of proceedings,* pp. 132–43.

Reprinted in Higginson, pp. 176–79.

1936

*578   'Changing Oxford' [letter], *New statesman and nation,* 5 Dec. 1936, pp. 888–89.

*579   'Communal supply of coal' [letter], *The Times,* 20 Nov. 1936, p. 12.

*580   'Danger to Oxford: invading cars: rubber paving in the "High": by-passes not enough', *Manchester guardian,* 12 Dec. 1936, p. 13.

*581   'Dr Mendelssohn Bartholdy', *The Times,* 1 Dec. 1936, p. 11.

582   'Henry Moore' [letter], *New Statesman and nation,* 14 Nov. 1936, p. 769.

*583 'An inquest on examinations', in *Conference of Educational Associations, held at University College London: twenty-fourth annual report, 1936* (London: [n.d.]), pp. 147–52.

*584 'Mgr Barnes', *The Times*, 16 Nov. 1936, p. 14.

*585 'Personal freedom: Sir Michael Sadler's view' [letter], *Anglo-German review*, 1 (1936), 60.

*586 'Preface', p. vii, to *Lady Barn House and the work of W. H. Herford*, by W. C. R. Hicks, Publications of the University of Manchester, 251, Educational series, 14 (Manchester: Manchester University Press, 1936).

*587 'Preface', pp. vii–xix [with P. J. Hartog], to *The marks of examiners, being a comparison of marks allotted to examination scripts by independent examiners and boards of examiners ...*, by Sir Philip Hartog and E. C. Rhodes (London: Macmillan, [for the] International Institute Examinations Enquiry, 1936).

*588 'The scholarship system in England to 1890', in *Essays on examinations* [with A. Abbott and others] (London: Macmillan, [for the] International Institute Examinations Enquiry, 1936), pp. 1–78.

Sadler also contributed (pp. 143–50) 'The leaving examination as conducted in the secondary schools of Prussia', reprinted from the *Report of the Royal Commission on Secondary Education* (1895), pp. 27–33 (no. 44 above).

*589 'Sir Algernon Firth', *The Times*, 5 Nov. 1936, p. 16.

*590 'Sir Charles Holmes', *The Times*, 10 Dec. 1936, p. 19.

591 'Sir Michael Sadler's tribute', *Oxford times*, 18 Dec. 1936, p. 32.
Obituary tribute to Rev. L. R. Phelps.

1937

592 'Forestry on the fells: playing havoc with a masterpiece' [letter], *Daily telegraph*, 13 Dec. 1937, p. 12.

*593 'Introduction', pp. v–viii, to *War of ideas in Spain: philosophy, politics and education,* by José Castillejo (London: Murray, 1937).

*594 'John Constable', *Burlington magazine,* 70 (1937), 261.

*595 'Mr John Russell', *The Times,* 18 Jan. 1937, p. 14.

*596 *Notes on a collection of English drawings [in the] Cooper Art Gallery, Barnsley* (Oxford: University Press, 1937). 46 pp.; plates.

*597 'Preface', p. xi [with P. J. Hartog], to *A conspectus of examinations in Great Britain and Northern Ireland,* by Sir Philip Hartog, with the assistance of Gladys Roberts (London: Macmillan, [for the] International Institute Examinations Enquiry, 1937).

*598 'Rousseau walks the earth', *University of Toronto quarterly,* 6 (1936–37), 151–58.
      Reprinted in Higginson, pp. 185–87.

*599 'Rousseau's "Emile" ' [letter], *The Times,* 11 Jan. 1937, p. 15.

*600 'Russell and Pestalozzi', *Times educational supplement,* 23 Jan. 1937, pp. 25–26.

1938

*601 [Appreciation of the work of Wassily Kandinsky, in the catalogue of Kandinsky's exhibition at the Guggenheim Jeune gallery, Cork Street, London W.1, 1938, p. 4.]

*602 'Certificates in secondary schools should be awarded by the teachers', *Schoolmaster,* 15 Dec. 1938, pp. 937, 951.

*603 'Dr Lascelles Abercrombie', *The Times,* 4 Nov. 1938, p. 16.

*604 'The examination system: school certificate' [letter], *The Times,* 6 Dec. 1938, p. 10.

*605   'A letter ... to Contemporary Lithographs', in *Catalogue of an exhibition of lithographs in colour published by Contemporary Lithographs Ltd*, [*at*] *Ernest Brown & Phillips, The Leicester Galleries, Leicester Square, 1938*, pp. [2–3].

*606   'Machinery of defence' [letter], *The Times*, 22 Nov. 1938, p. 10.

*607   'Mr John Henderson', *The Times*, 24 Nov. 1938, p. 16.

608   'Notes on the way', *Time and tide*, 29 Oct. 1938, pp. 1484–86.

609   'An old Oxford house' [letter], *Oxford mail*, 12 Dec. 1938, p. 4.

610   'A show house for Oxford' [letter], *Oxford times*, 25 Nov. 1938, p. 6.

*611   'Sir Brajendranath Seal', *The Times*, 6 Dec. 1938, p. 16.

612   'To communism via civil war' [letter], *Time and tide*, 12 Nov. 1938, p. 1562.

613   'Two-mindedness in foreign policy' [letter], *Time and tide*, 15 Oct. 1938, pp. 1424–25.

*614   'Why make all children go to school?' [letter], *Times educational supplement*, 17 Dec. 1938, pp. 457–58.

1939

*615   'Art in education: IX, Conclusion and comment', *Listener*, 28 Sept. 1939, pp. 614–16.

*616   'Chinese universities' [letter, with A. G. Castleton], *The Times*, 7 Jan. 1939, p. 8.

*617   [Review of Arthur Mayhew, *Education in the colonial empire* (London, 1938)], in *Africa*, 12 (1939), 108–11.

*618 'Sir Alfred Hopkinson', *The Times*, 15 Nov. 1939, p. 11.

*619 'Sir Ernest Bain', *The Times*, 27 Nov. 1939, p. 8.

1940

*620 'Lady Rhondda's "Notes on the way" ' [letter], *Time and tide,* 14 Dec. 1940, p. 1230.

*621 'Post-war settlement' [letter], *Time and tide,* 28 Dec. 1940, p. 1272.

1941

*622 'The arts in English education after the war', *Athene,* 1 (1941), 8–10.

*623 'Christchurch meadow' [letter], *The Times,* 18 Oct. 1941, p. 5.

*624 'Dr P. Sandiford: an appreciation', *Manchester guardian,* 18 Oct. 1941, p. 8.

*625 'In grateful retrospect', *Journal of education,* 73 (1941), 474–75.

*626 'Juncta disjuncta: I, The English public schools; II, Future of the private schools; III, "The troubled sea of the mind"; IV, The two-mindedness of England about education; V, A ministry of health and education', *Times educational supplement,* 20 & 27 Sept., 4, 11 & 18 Oct. 1941, pp. 445, 457, 471, 483, 495.

> Reprinted by *The Times* as an 8-page pamphlet, 1941. 'The two-mindedness of England about education' is reprinted in Higginson, pp. 187–89.

*627 'Preface', pp. v–viii [with P. J. Hartog], to *The marking of English essays: a report on an investigation carried out by a sub-committee of the International Institute Examinations Enquiry Committee,* consisting of Sir Philip Hartog (Chairman) . . . [and others] (London: Macmillan, [for the] International Institute Examinations Enquiry, 1941).

*628 'The Rev. Thory G. Gardiner', *The Times*, 6 Nov. 1941, p. 7.

*629 'Victorian Oxford', *Times educational supplement*, 25 Oct. 1941, p. 506.

> A review of Sir Charles Oman, *Memories of Victorian Oxford and of some early years* (London, 1941). Unsigned.

1942

*630 'Centenary of Thomas Arnold: statesman and prophet', *Times educational supplement*, 13 June 1942, p. 281.

1944

631 *"K": a breviate of the life and work of Eva Margaret Gilpin, 1869–1940* (Welwyn Garden City, 1944). 55 pp.

> A posthumous publication, privately printed.

Subject index

The index is primarily intended to act as a finding-list for Sadler's publications. It does not pretend to index the contents of his writings, being compiled in almost all cases from the titles alone. Personal names are generally as given in the publications.